Helmut Wick

Helmut Wick

An Illustrated Biography of the Luftwaffe Ace and Commander of *Jagdgeschwader 2* during the Battle of Britain

Herbert Ringlstetter

Schiffer Military History
Atglen, PA

Translated from the German by David Johnston
Book Design by Ian Robertson.

Library of Congress Control Number: 2004114859

Printed in China.
ISBN: 0-7643-2217-6

This book was originally printed under the title,
Major Helmut Wick: Kommodore Jagdgeschwader Richthofen Nr. 2
by Motorbuch Verlag

Published by Schiffer Publishing Ltd.
4880 Lower Valley Road
Atglen, PA 19310
Phone: (610) 593-1777
FAX: (610) 593-2002
E-mail: info@schifferbooks.com.
Visit our web site at: www.schifferbooks.com
Please write for a free catalog.
This book may be purchased from the publisher.
Please include $3.95 postage.
Try your bookstore first.

In Europe, Schiffer books are distributed by:
Bushwood Books
6 Marksbury Avenue
Kew Gardens
Surrey TW9 4JF
England
Phone: 44 (0) 20 8392-8585
FAX: 44 (0) 20 8392-9876
E-mail: info@bushwoodbooks.co.uk.
Free postage in the UK. Europe: air mail at cost.
Try your bookstore first.

Contents

In memory of Helmut Wick
and the fliers of all nations who lost their lives
in World War II.

Foreword

In the summer and autumn of 1940, Helmut Wick rose to become one of the great heroes of the German air force. Germany's most worthy soldiers were awarded the highest level of the Iron Cross, the Knight's Cross, as a visible sign of courage and bravery. The Oak Leaves, created on 3 June 1940 and awarded just seven times in 1940, brought those who wore it fame and honor equaled in peacetime only by great actors. In 1940 Helmut Wick became the fourth member of the German armed services (*Wehrmacht*) to receive the Knight's Cross with Oak Leaves. In just three months he rose from an *Oberleutnant* in command of a squadron (*Staffel*) to a *Major* in command of an entire fighter wing (*Jagdgeschwader*), and this at the age of 25! Such a rise would have been unthinkable in peacetime. But his meteoric rise was abruptly cut short. On 28 November 1940 his career unexpectedly came to a tragic end; the seemingly invulnerable "Siegfried" of the German fighter arm failed to return from a combat mission. In Helmut Wick the *Luftwaffe* lost one of its best fighter pilots. His wife, however, lost her husband, his one-year-old son lost his father, and his unborn daughter lost the opportunity to ever know her father. For many fighter pilots, especially those of the *"Richthofen" Geschwader*, Wick was a role model and dependable comrade. But he also had his critics—his quick, daredevil style of attacking the enemy did not lend itself well to large-scale, prudent operations, especially in *Geschwader* strength.

This book is based on the writings of Franz Fiby, who flew 110 missions with his friend and comrade Helmut Wick. In graphic style, the passages from Franz Fiby's diary provide an insight into the life of young fighter pilots of 1939 and 1940. These young men had but one task: to shoot down other young men men who were just like them, except that they were of a different nationality. Helmut Wick was one of those men, who lived a life in keeping with and inextricably linked to that fateful time—Helmut Wick was not a self-made hero; instead, it was the conditions of the war and his era that were largely responsible for what he became.

Landshut, 2000
Herbert Ringlstetter

Major WICK

28 November 1940

Northern France, Querqueville, near Cherbourg—one of the most important forward airfields of *Jagdgeschwader "Richthofen" Nr. 2*. It is Thursday, 28 November 1940. Fine days have become rare, but today the sun smiles on Normandy and the Channel. In the early afternoon 31 Messerschmitt Bf 109s of JG 2 once again set out for England and encounter Spitfires. The staff flight (*Stabsschwarm*), consisting of *Oberleutnant* Rudolf Pflanz, *Leutnant* Franz Fiby, *Oberleutnant* Erich Leie, and *Major* Helmut Wick shoots down two enemy aircraft—Leie's 11th and Wick's 55th victories.

At 1635 hours elements of JG 2 take off on another mission over the Channel. Leading the way is the *Stabsschwarm*. The French mainland gradually disappears as the Messerschmitt fighters climb into the blue sky. Visibility is excellent. Approximately 100 kilometers of water lie between the French and British coasts.

Approximately 1710 hours. The Germans are flying at a height of 10500 meters south of the Isle of Wight when English fighters appear above them. *Major* Wick immediately applies full power so as to achieve a favorable attack position as quickly as possible. The *Stabsschwarm* and the rest of the *Geschwader* try to keep up, but become widely spread out by the maneuver. In his usual daredevil style, Wick plunges into the enemy formation and latches onto the tail of a Spitfire. Wick opens fire with his cannon and machine-guns, and his 56th goes down. Seconds later Wick himself is fired on. He dives away. In the ensuing dogfight *Oberleutnant* Pflanz loses sight of the *Stabsschwarm* and his wingman, *Leutnant* Fiby. After contacting Fiby by radio, Pflanz heads for France alone. Then, some distance away, he sees two aircraft that he initially takes for Bf 109s, also returning to France. As he moves closer, however, he is surprised to see the aircraft behind firing at the one in front. The Spitfire shoots down the Messerschmitt, whose pilot bails out. Pflanz moves in behind the Spitfire, whose pilot is probably still watching the doomed Messerschmitt. It is a fatal mistake. Pflanz fires at the British fighter, which crashes into the water with its pilot, not far from where the Messerschmitt went in. He then radios the *Luftwaffe*'s air-sea rescue service, hoping that the downed German pilot might yet be saved. JG 2's fighters return to France. Only one Bf 109 is overdue—that of the *Kommodore*, *Major* Helmut Wick. No one knows for sure what happened. Perhaps the *Kommodore* has landed somewhere else and might yet report in. And if he did come down in the "Brook," perhaps the Tommies have picked him up. Everyone hopes for good news. Wick is surely still alive, perhaps injured, drifting in the cold water of the Channel. But the sea is rough, and it is beginning to get dark.

When *Reichsmarschall* Hermann Göring, Commander-in-Chief of the *Luftwaffe*, hears of the incident, he orders torpedo boats to go out into the night and look for Wick. But they have no luck. The next day light naval vessels and aircraft of the air-sea rescue service, escorted by Messerschmitt fighters of JG 2, search for the missing *Kommodore*. Two oil patches are sighted on the surface of the water, but nothing else. *Major* Wick is never found, and his fate remains unexplained to this day.

Childhood and Youth

Swapokmund, German Southwest Africa, 1914. Karl Wick is a civil engineer working for a large German company. His wife has accompanied him to the German protectorate. After three years they are planning a lengthy vacation at home. As well, Frau Wick is expecting her second child, and she wants it to be born in her homeland. With her son Walter, who was born in Swapokmund, she sails to Germany. Frau Wick plans to spend her vacation in the Taunus Region and Mannheim, her home town. Her husband follows two months later. The Wicks never return to Southwest Africa, however—the outbreak of the First World War shatters their plans. They are forced to leave everything they have behind in Swapokmund. The Wick family settles in Rohrbach, near Heidelberg. Daughter Doris is born, and one year later, on 5 August 1915, their second son, Helmut Paul Emil, is born in Mannheim. Helmut later stated that he wished he had been born in Africa like his brother Walter and grown up there.

The Wick family. On the left beside his mother is little Helmut, right his older siblings Walter and Doris.

Helmut at age 15 in Königsberg.

The Wick children saw little of their father, as he was kept busy building roads and bridges, work vital to the war effort.

The war ended, and in 1919 the family moved, this time to a house in the country, near Hanover. The three children were happy there, until the sad day in February 1922 when they lost their mother. It was a fateful blow that would affect Helmut for the rest of his life. Their father took the children to Danzig, where a new job awaited him and memories of their mother were not so omnipresent. One of their mother's sisters took over the housekeeping, but of course she could never take her place. Herr Wick built a house for his family in Oliva, near Danzig. There was plenty there to keep the Wick children busy: bicycling, swimming, hiking, and skiing. Right next to the site where the company run by his father stored its building materials was Danzig-Langfuhr airfield. There young Helmut made his first acquaintance with flying. His father bought him a flight in a commercial aircraft. The experience left an indelible mark on the young man. Soon afterward his father remarried. It was a move that the three Wick children welcomed.

At the beginning of 1929 the Wick family moved again, this time to Königsberg, in East Prussia. There, to Helmut's joy, his father bought an automobile. He also leased a hunting property. For the youngest Wick son it was the beginning of a passion that would never leave him. He stalked deer for hours, and this, together with his love of everything to do with the forest, led him to consider a career as a forester. Helmut also seems to have been infected with the "Flying Virus," however. His father bought him another flight, and this time he was permitted to take the controls. It was a turning point. His desire to become a forester waned, and from then on Helmut dreamed of becoming a commercial pilot.

I Want to Become a Pilot

In 1935 the Wicks moved again, this time to Berlin. There he graduated from high school. His brother Walter had meanwhile become an officer candidate in the 1st Artillery Regiment. After the *Führer* announced the formation of a new air force, Helmut made up his mind: he no longer wanted to be a commercial pilot; instead, he would become a fighter pilot. So in the spring of 1935 he applied to the officer candidate selection office in Berlin. Helmut scored well on the suitability tests and was accepted. His training as an officer and pilot was scheduled to begin in spring 1936. That was a long time to wait, especially for an impatient young man, but Wick did not have much time for casual pursuits, as the Labor Service came calling. The young man had to be satisfied with a shovel until he finally got his hand on what he truly desired—the control stick of an aircraft.

Helmut Wick began his military service at the *Luftwaffe* officer candidate school in Dresden on 6 April 1936, and on 16 April he swore the oath of allegiance to Adolf Hitler. Flying was not part of the program in the beginning; instead, the aspiring pilots exercised, attended theoretical lectures, and trained with firearms. Officer Candidate Wick stuck to it, and on 13 July he was assessed as "well suited to become an officer."

A Focke-Wulf Fw 44 "*Stieglitz*" (Goldfinch). This docile machine was ideally suited for basic flight training. Helmut Wick learned to fly on this type.

Budding pilots study a map, memorizing the location of the training area for an upcoming aerobatics flight.

***Fähnrich* Wick in 1938. At that time his performance left something to be desired.**

Flight cadets in Dresden. Helmut Wick is in the front, third from the left.

***Oberfähnrich* Wick in 1938.**

Flight training now began in earnest. Wick soon soloed, an unforgettable experience for every pilot, in a Focke-Wulf "*Stieglitz*" biplane.

Wick did not display extraordinary talent during training; he was assessed as an average pilot. He had difficulty with his theoretical studies. As in school, Helmut had difficulty learning things that were of little or no interest to him. His success also depended to a great extent on who was teaching him. At the beginning of May 1937 he was temporarily attached to the *6. Staffel* of bomber unit 254. Even though it was not a fighter unit, Wick experienced life in an operational unit for the first time. One month later he returned to the officer candidate school in Dresden. His performance remained the same as before: if he wasn't particularly interested in a subject or it seemed too theoretical, his enthusiasm was limited.

Things were even worse on the third course. The following is from an overall assessment made after his intermediate examination:

"Small in stature, not yet military enough in appearance. Excellent character. Not always clear in his manner, very reserved. Still not a complete personality. Must become stronger mentally and develop a better concept of duty. At present he still requires supervision. Talented, but his performance depends on his interest in a subject. He must become more diligent and constant. Above average physically and militarily, below average as a pilot, indifferent and lacking in zeal. Appearance and deportment satisfactory. Wick's performance in the intermediate examination is rated unsatisfactory, especially in terms of personality. It is unlikely that he will be able to successfully

The Arado Ar 68, here an aircraft of 6./JG 334. Together with the Heinkel He 51, it formed the standard equipment of the new *Luftwaffe's* fighter units. It was eventually replaced by the vastly superior Bf 109.

Two Messerschmitt Bf 109 D fighters of JG 53 wearing the standard prewar paint scheme.

***Hauptmann* Werner Mölders. Under his proverbial fatherly leadership, Helmut Wick received outstanding fighter pilot training.**

complete the course. Based on his aptitude and personality, however, he is found worthy of another chance to prove his ability. A second course promises success."

Wick was given a second chance to pass the third course, reporting to the officer candidate school in Wildpark-Werder on 1 April 1938. He successfully completed the course, and in the summer of 1938 reported to the Fighter Training School in Werneuchen. The prospective pilots went through a six-week course of training tailored specifically to produce fighter pilots. At Werneuchen *Fähnrich* Wick attracted attention on account of his excellent shooting and his aggressive, daredevil style, even though his attacks were a little sloppy. After completing fighter school, Wick was transferred to a proper fighter unit, *Jagdgeschwader 333* under *Oberstleutnant* Max Ibel, which was based in Herzogenaurach. Assigned to the *I. Gruppe*, he flew the Arado Ar 68, an obsolete biplane. Conversion to the modern Messerschmitt Bf 109 was still in the future.

On 8 November 1938 *Oberfähnrich* Wick was promoted to *Leutnant*, and on 1 January 1939 he was transferred to Wiesbaden to the *1. Staffel* of JG 133. Somewhat later, in May of the same year, the *Geschwader* was renamed JG 53.

It took a while for Wick to adjust. To his great good fortune, in March 1939 Werner Mölders returned from the Spanish Civil War. With 14 victories, he was the most successful fighter pilot in the "*Legion Condor*," the German intervention force. *Hauptmann* Mölders

Summer 1939. Werner "Daddy" Mölders (seventh from right) with his men. Wick is second from the left.

was placed in command of the *1. Staffel*. Mölders had a knack for teaching his men the fine art of aerial combat. No theory could replace his experiences in Spain. Mölders provided the understanding that was so vital in teaching something to Wick. Under Mölders' tutelage Wick became a flight leader (*Schwarmführer*). Wick and Mölders got along well, even though their natures were completely different. Looking back, in late August 1940 Helmut Wick spoke of these times to a war correspondent:

"When I joined 1./JG 53 as a young Leutnant I was, as we are fond of saying, the lowest of the low. Major Mölders, who wore the Spanish Cross with Diamonds, at that time already the Ace of Aces, made me what I am today. Mölders trained us tirelessly, conducting realistic air combat training based on his wealth of experience. When, after four weeks as a wingman I'd had it drilled into me sufficiently on the airfield, he gave me a number of chances—he let me loose on the enemy. I will be grateful to Mölders for that as long as I live. Mölders was the only instructor I ever had who embodied the qualities of the perfect teacher and superior, together with those of the ideal comrade. He was a role model for every fighter pilot who ever flew with him. In any case, he is my role model during every second of every mission. I would even go so far as to say that he was the one who turned me into a usable officer and fighter pilot. That time in Major Janson's Gruppe and Hauptmann Mölders' Staffel had a decisive impact on my subsequent success."

There were also changes in Wick's private life. On 3 August Wick's commanding officer gave him permission to marry, which was then required for young officers. Helmut traveled to Berlin where, on his birthday, he married 23-year-old Ursula Rolfs.

The Real Thing - the Outbreak of War

Much to Helmut Wick's regret, on 31 August 1939 he was transferred to JG 2 *"Richthofen,"* based at Döberitz, near Berlin. He joined the unit's *3. Staffel* on 1 September 1939, the very day German forces invaded Poland. At that time the *Richthofen Geschwader* was under the command of *Oberst* Gerd von Massow. *Leutnant* Wick was assigned a Messerschmitt Bf 109 E-3 bearing the tactical code "Yellow 3."

Many of the youthful fighter pilots were disappointed that JG 2 took no part in the fighting in Poland; instead, it was assigned to protect the capital. Soon the first reports were received of enemy aircraft shot down by other units. Even his old unit, the *I. Gruppe* of JG 53, which was defending Germany's border with France, reported victories. Helmut was annoyed. the *"Richthofen" Geschwader* never sighted a single enemy aircraft during the fighting in Poland. *Oberst* Massow, who was a friend of *Luftwaffe* Commander-in-Chief Göring, asked the *Generalfeldmarschall* to have his unit transferred to the west. Göring responded favorably, and the *Geschwader* was transferred to Frankfurt-Rebstock. The *Geschwader*'s new mission was to defend Germany's western frontier, and the pilots hoped that they would soon see action. The unit's fighters were to patrol the frontier, but any violation of the French border was strictly forbidden, for Germany's leaders were still hopeful that England and France might come to terms.

JG 2 patrolled day in, day out, and soon the routine became boring. Still there was no sign of the enemy. In a letter home Helmut wrote:

"So far I, indeed the entire Gruppe, have yet to see an enemy aircraft. I am definitely hopeful, however, that I will shoot down at least one of the enemy before the war is over."

Above: Döberitz air base near Berlin, home to JG *"Richthofen"* Nr. 2. Opposite: Gerd von Massow, *Kommodore* of *Jagdgeschwader "Richthofen" Nr. 2* from autumn 1936 until March 1940.

"One of Them Must go Down!" Wick's First Victory

22 November 1939. The *3. Staffel*'s third *Schwarm*, consisting of *Leutnant* Wick, *Feldwebel* Jaenisch, *Leutnant* Votel, and *Leutnant* Fiby, is once again on patrol along the border. It is Wick's sixth combat mission. Taking advantage of a favorable wind, the young men in the Messerschmitts allow themselves to be carried over the French border. Suddenly a cluster of tiny dots appears above them—it can only be enemy aircraft. Two of the dots separate from the rest. As they come nearer Wick recognizes them as French Curtiss fighters. The Germans dive away with the French in pursuit. Helmut Wick described this encounter:

"As I headed back up in a climbing turn I saw a Frenchman behind me. I remember vividly seeing his cockades as I looked back. It was one of the strangest moments of my life, and I admit that the sight of those red, white, and blue rings put me into a bit of a funk. The Frenchman was also blazing away at me. To know that he was sitting on my tail shooting at me was extremely uncomfortable. Finally, my first air combat. Just in time I remembered what the master teacher Mölders had told me: when in a ticklish situation, always withdraw first and then observe. I stood my bird on its nose, and I was so much faster than the Frenchman in the dive that I was able to shake him off quickly. When I could no longer see the enemy aircraft, I was sure that the others would be above me on the left, but there was no one there. Could they be to the right? When I looked behind on the right, I couldn't believe my eyes. I was looking right into four radial engines, from which small red flames were spurting. Immediately and unconsciously, as happens in such situations, a ridiculous thought flashed through my head: are they allowed to just shoot at me like that? Equally quickly I considered what to do: run away again? No, this time attack, and one of them must go down! I clenched my teeth, pushed the stick to the right, and applied full right rudder. When I had completed the turn, the first one flew past right in front of me. The second was close behind, and I approached him head-on. The sight of his guns firing was horrible. We were too close to each other to have any effect. He flashed overhead, and then the third one was there, just as close as the second. I made a slight course correction to get him in my sight and aimed as they had taught us in school. When I opened fire I saw several pieces of metal fly off the Frenchman, and then both wings broke off. Close behind him came the fourth Curtiss, which also fired at me. In all of this my machine did not sustain a single hit. The first two climbed back up, and I did the same to prevent them from overtaking me. It was time for me to head home, as my fuel was running low. I looked around and saw that I was all alone. My wingman, who returned to base before me, had become separated from me during the dogfight. I encountered no more Frenchmen during the flight home, and I was not upset about it."

Still stirred up from combat, Wick lost his way and had to land at another airfield for fuel. Finally he returned to base, where he was able to make a low pass while waggling his wings to announce his victory. After landing he was so excited over his victory and the joy on the airfield that he tried several times to climb out of the cockpit before releasing his harness.

Another *Schwarm* from the *3. Staffel* had also made contact with enemy aircraft, and *Oberfeldwebel* Kley had claimed one shot down. These were the *Geschwader*'s first successes, for which Wick and Kley were awarded the Iron Cross, Second Class. *Oberfeldwebel* Kley, who had scored the first victory, also received a gold watch from the *Kommodore*.

The Curtiss shot down by *Leutnant* Wick was probably flown by *Sergent* Saillard, who was killed in action.

The winter of 1939-40 was very cold, but the fighters had to be kept at a constant state of readiness, which was not always easy for the "Black Men" of the ground personnel.

Helmut went home for Christmas and New Years. Waiting for him there were his parents and his wife, Ursel, but also his son, Walter, who had been born the previous October. Life within the circle of his family lasted just a few weeks, however, after which Helmut rejoined his *Gruppe* at Frankfurt-Rebstock.

JG 2, including *Hauptmann* Henning Strümpell's *3. Staffel*, continued flying border patrols. When asked about Wick for this book, Strümpell told the author:

"Wick didn't really stand out until the offensive in the west. He was well liked and a good pilot, but at that time I had many good pilots in my Staffel. It wasn't until encounters with the enemy became more frequent that he began to stand out more. He was a real daredevil."

There were no further combats in the months that followed, however. Leave interrupted the boredom, and he spent 10-17 February in the Black Forest. Six places were reserved for the pilots of the *Richthofen Geschwader* in the Opel House on the Feldberg, and the *Staffeln* visited in turns. As *Staffelkapitän* Strümpell situated himself in the "Feldberger Hof," a total of three officers and four non-commissioned officers were able to go. The seven young men arrived after a 12-hour journey. Most spent their days on the slopes, and *Leutnant* Wick proved an extremely capable skier. In the evenings they sat with other guests or on their own, drinking champagne. A coin toss usually decided who would buy the next bottle. The young men wore casual civilian attire, which was usually preferred to uniform while on sporting leave.

After a pleasant week in the Black Forest it was back to Frankfurt-Rebstock. The weather was fine on 18 February, so Wick and his *Staffel* mates were back in their machines. During one mission the Messerschmitt fighters climbed to an altitude of more than 8000 meters. Their sorties remained uneventful, however, until 9 March. The weather was poor, with a solid cloud deck and haze restricting visibility. The mission order was: seek out enemy reconnaissance machines over the front. Seven Bf 109s climbed into the sky. Wick was in temporary command of the *Staffel*. As the flight proceeded the weather improved visibly. After 65 minutes in the air heavy anti-aircraft fire was sighted—German anti-aircraft fire. Seconds later French aircraft appeared, 11 Morane 406 fighters and

Bf 109 Es at Frankfurt-Rebstock. Along with Bassenheim, this was one of I./JG 2's main bases from November 1939 until mid-May 1940.

Servicing the engine of a Bf 109 E at Frankfurt-Rebstock.

The winter of 1939-40 was a hard one, with heavy snow well into March. Here the *Kapitän* of the *3. Staffel*, *Hauptmann* Strümpell, addresses his men before a mission on 14 March.

Above: Fueling a Bf 109 E-1 of the *3. Staffel*.

Right: A portable heater is used to preheat the Daimler-Benz motor of one of JG 2's Messerschmitts.

Below: Members of the ground crew move an aircraft of the *Geschwaderstab*.

Leutnant Wick in winter flight suit and helmet.

Below and facing page: *Hauptmann* Strümpell and his aircraft "Yellow 1." The aircraft number has been crudely removed by the censor. The "Horrido" pennant, Strümpell's personal emblem, may be seen on the engine cowling. The pale blue pennant had its origins in a hunting club in Pomerania. *Oberleutnant der Reserve* Kieckebusch stayed at the Pomera-

nian estate several times in 1938, establishing a link between it and the officers of the *3. Staffel*. During one such visit, the Horrido pennant was given to Strümpell, who mounted it on his private automobile for a time. After war broke out, he had the emblem painted on his Bf 109. The other pilots liked the emblem, and from the spring of 1940 it began appearing on most of the *3. Staffel's* machines. The black top hat is a reference to Strümpell's service with the Legion Condor in Spain. The top hat emblem was an original creation of Hannes Trautloft.

A Bf 109 E takes off in a cloud of snow.

Leutnant Franz Fiby in the cockpit of a Bf 109. Fiby kept a detailed diary, and readers of this book are indebted to him for much of the information contained herein.

Winter 1939-40: a pair of Messerschmitt Bf 109s takes off on a patrol flight along the French border.

Wearing a heavy winter flight suit—captured from the Czechs—Franz Fiby clambers from the cockpit of "Yellow 13," which he often flew at this time. His personal aircraft "Yellow 14" was assigned to him in mid-March 1940.

two twin-engined Potez 63s. *Leutnant* Wick stalked the enemy aircraft. He nosed over and dove on the enemy, but his aim was poor. The attack was rushed and lacked concentration. His wingman, *Leutnant* Fiby, also had bad luck. He was so excited that he forgot to fire his cannon, using only his machine-guns. Fuel was running low and a long flight home lay ahead, so Wick broke off the attack. For safety's sake the fighters stopped at Wiesbaden, after 95 minutes flying time. From there it was just 15 minutes back to Rebstock. There the *Staffel* was celebrating. *Feldwebel* Jaenisch had claimed an enemy aircraft shot down, and at least two other French machines had been hit.

In the days and weeks that followed conditions at the front remained the same. Encounters between German and French aircraft were rare. This did not suit Wick, who hoped to soon meet the enemy again, use the lessons he had learned, and gain another victory.

His next opportunity to add to his score came quite unexpectedly on 30 April. Wick's *Schwarm* took off from Bassenheim for the purpose of tuning their radios. Everything seemed quite peaceful, rather like a Sunday outing. In spite of this, of course, the pilots armed their guns. The four Messerschmitts had already begun the turn towards home when Wick spotted a twin-engined aircraft above them. The others saw it as well. *Leutnant* Pflanz called out "Do 17!", while *Leutnant* Fiby identified it as a Bf 110. Suddenly the French cockades became visible in the sun. "Potez!" called Wick. The French pilot put his nose down and attempted to flee, but the German fighters were much faster. They soon overtook the enemy machine. Pflanz and Wick were the first to close the range. The pilot of the Potez flew well, but against four Messerschmitt Bf 109s his situation was almost hopeless. The fate of the French machine was settled in a few minutes. Ablaze, it smashed into the ground. None of the three crewman were able to get out—all died in their machine.

The Germans were doubly pleased about the victory, as the French reconnaissance aircraft had been operating in the area for quite a while and regularly attacked German positions on their way home.

As all four members of the *Schwarm* participated in the shooting down of the Potez, it was credited to the *3. Staffel* rather than to one individual. It was Rudi Pflanz, however, who probably fired the decisive burst.

Fighter pilots of JG 2 photographed in January 1940 during a ski vacation on the Feldberg. From the left: *Unteroffizier* Stritzel, *Leutnant* Fiby, unidentified, *Hauptmann* Strümpell, *Leutnant* Wick, *Feldwebel* Specht, and *Feldwebel* Jaenisch.

Coffee break at Frankfurt-Rebstock at the beginning of March 1940. From left: *Leutnant* Wick, *Feldwebel* Jaenisch, *Leutnant* Fiby, and *Feldwebel* Hücher.

Left: Perhaps not his day—in the photo, at least, *Leutnant* Wick appears tired and worn out.

Below: *Gefreiter* Günter Seeger (left), a member of 2./JG 2 since late February 1940, studying enemy aircraft recognition cards with *Leutnant* Wick and *Unteroffizier* Stritzel.

***

May 10th saw the beginning of the long-awaited German offensive in the west. For the fighter pilots, too, it was the beginning of a period of intensive operations. Often several missions were flown in one day. The units moved frequently to keep pace with the advance. Sometimes the army moved so quickly that the *Luftwaffe* was unable to keep up. The heroic airmen of the French air force fought with determination, however, they suffered from incompetent leadership. The Royal Air Force sent pilots and aircraft to France, but these were unable to alter the course of events.

Wick's "Yellow 2" went unserviceable at the start of the French campaign with engine trouble. With no other aircraft available, he was forced to remain on the ground. This annoyed the ambitious *Leutnant*, especially when his fellow pilots returned from an action against Blenheims of the RAF and claimed five victories.

Two days later, however, Wick was back in the air. On 17 May he succeeded in shooting down three LeO 45s, modern twin-engined bombers produced by Lioré et Olivier. Two days later Wick was successful again. Near Calais he shot down two Fairey Swordfish, British biplane torpedo bombers. They were relatively easy prey, but Wick's claims were not confirmed, as there was no one to witness his victories. The *Wehrmacht* rolled through France with an ease that no one could have imagined. Germany had firm control of the skies. The fighters were given a wide variety of missions: free chases, fighter escort, and defensive patrols over bridges and roads. The boredom was long gone.

On 5 June Wick scored a then unprecedented four victories in one mission. Four times he thundered over the airfield, rocking his wings to signal his victories. So vigorous were his maneuvers that the mechanics feared that the undercarriage might not lower. On 6 June Wick became the first pilot of the *I. Gruppe* to complete 100 combat missions. The ground personnel gave him a warm welcome and a large bouquet of flowers. He also claimed two more victories, his 9th and 10th.

For this feat *Leutnant* Wick was awarded the iron Cross, First Class by *Oberstleutnant* Harry von Bülow-Bothkamp, the *Geschwaderkommodore*. Wick should have received the decoration sooner, however, his victories were simply too fast for the German bureaucracy.

Twelve victory bars adorned the rudder of Wick's Bf 109 when a minor parking mishap resulted in the loss of the aircraft. The fighter rolled down a slope and was heavily damaged. The ground crewman responsible was inconsolable, and Wick was severely crestfallen over the loss of his faithful kite.

His new aircraft, an E-4, was also coded "Yellow 2." Wick's personal emblem, a small bird, was painted on the left side of the aircraft's fuselage. The bird may have been a kingfisher, a nimble, skilled hunter. It was also seen as a good luck charm. The emblem may also have had something to do with Wick's son, little Walter, who symbolically flew with Wick as a "Little Bird."

By the end of the campaign in the west Wick's victory total stood at 14. This made him the high scorer of JG 2, followed by *Oberfeldwebel* Machold of the *III. Gruppe* with 11. The most successful German fighter pilot at that time was *Hauptmann* Mölders of JG 53, who had been taken prisoner by the French on 5 June, with 25 victories. *Hauptmann* Balthasar of JG 27 had 23 victories, while *Hauptmann* Gentzen, who had enjoyed much success over Poland, had been killed in May after 18 victories. At the end of June *Oberleutnant* Paul Temme, *I. Gruppe* adjutant, and *Oberleutnant* Kieckbusch took off in a four-seat Bf 108 to look for a new base for the *Gruppe*. They found it just beyond the small town of Beaumont-le-Roger, about 40 km southwest of Rouen. The site was a grain field, and its broad, flat surface seemed ideally suited for this purpose. Soon afterward a *Schwarm* from the *3. Staffel* led by *Leutnant* Wick circled over the field. Franz Jaenisch was first to land his Messerschmitt on the soon to be forward airfield. The others followed, but the grain was a meter and a half tall, and the aircraft could not take off again. The four pilots had to wait for the ground crews to flatten everything with their vehicles. Barracks were erected for the new airfield's personnel, and the *II. Gruppe* and the *Geschwaderstab* also moved to the new field. The command staff and many pilots were quartered in a small castle, the property of Princess Caraman-Chimay, wife of the Count de Magenta. Neither was asked for permission. One wing of the castle was left for their use, but the count and countess soon began working for the resistance, passing information to London.

The *3. Staffel* moved into the house of an artist who had fled a few days before the Germans arrived. Franz Fiby wrote in his diary:

"Our Staffel's pilots are now living in the house of an artist, the American painter Aston Knight. We really like it here, and on our days off we sit in a garden set up by the operations officer and feel like we're on vacation."

Spring 1940, on the small airfield at Bassenheim. From left: *Unteroffizier* Stritzel, *Leutnant* Wick, *Hauptmann* Strümpell, *Hauptmann* von Winterfeldt, *Leutnant* Pflanz, and *Feldwebel* Jaenisch.

Happy group at the "Café Archibald," Bassenheim, in the spring of 1940. Archibald was Strümpell's nickname. From left: Helmut Wick, Franz Jaenisch, unidentified, Fritz Stritzel, the young lady serving them, Henning "Archibald" Strümpell, and Rudi Pflanz.

Peering from the window of the "Café Archibald" on the airfield at Bassenfeld (from left: Jaenisch, unidentified, Strümpell, Pflanz). In the background is "Yellow 9," which also bears the Horrido pennant, recently adopted as the *3. Staffel's* emblem. In front of the window is the standard of 3./JG 2.

Helmut Wick and Günter Seeger are welcomed by the Staffel mascot. In the background are several of the *3. Staffel's* Bf 109s.

"Black Men" fueling a Bf 109 E of the *III. Gruppe* of JG 2.

Leutnant Wick with the Staffel's senior non-commissioned officer, *Oberfeldwebel* Carra.

Ground personnel of *7. Staffel*, JG 2, on the road in France, moving to the next airfield.

Morane-Saulnier M.S. 406 fighters of the French Air Force.

Above: Dewoitine 520. This modern French fighter was the equal of the Messerschmitt Bf 109 in most respects, but was only built in small numbers. Below: Hurricane pilots race to their aircraft on a French airfield, May 1940.

Above: Curtiss Hawk 75 fighters of the Armée de l'Air fly escort for Fairey Battles of the Royal Air Force. The Battle units suffered heavy casualties and were soon withdrawn from front-line service. Below: The remains of a Hurricane fighter on the beach at Dunkirk, following the evacuation of the British expeditionary corps.

...and a Spitfire.

There were also losses on the German side—here the burnt-out remains of a Bf 109.

Many French cities were heavily damaged in the fighting of 1940 and later by Allied bombing, resulting in casualties among the civilian population.

Large numbers of French aircraft were captured on former bases of the Armée de l'Air. Here is a seemingly intact Bloch 152 fighter.

Many other French aircraft were destroyed or damaged on the ground, like this Morane-Saulnier M.S. 406. The national emblem on the fuselage has apparently been removed as a souvenir.

Partially burnt-out Bloch 152. The bent platoon blades suggest that the aircraft crash-landed with the motor running.

June 1940 near Evreux. German mechanics fire up the radial engine of a Curtiss Hawk 75 A. In the background is a Bf 109 E of JG 2.

The Douglas DB-7 was a modern twin-engined bomber built in America. Small numbers of this type entered service with the French air force shortly before the surrender.

The Potez 65 served as a bomber and reconnaissance aircraft. These aircraft are not camouflaged, suggesting that they were rushed into service.

In the British Isles, meanwhile, there was still time to relax. Flying Officer John Dundas of No. 609 Squadron in the spring of 1940. The squadron was based at Drem in Scotland until May, when it was transferred to Northolt west of London. From July the unit operated from Middle Wallop and Warmwell, making a direct counterpart of JG 2.

Two Spitfire Mk Is of No. 609 Squadron, spring 1940. PR-O was flown by John Dundas. On 7 October the aircraft was damaged in combat with Bf 110s and Dundas was obliged to make a forced landing at Warmwell. Despite a leg injury, he resumed flying the next day.

Above: June 1940—a pilot of the *3. Staffel* lies in the grass enjoying the spring sun as he waits for the order to go into action. In the background is Wick's first "Yellow 2". Note that the pale blue finish on the fuselage sides has already been overpainted. The aircraft wears the Horrido pennant and 12 victory bars on its tail.

Center: An armorer works on the 7.9-mm MG 17 machine-guns mounted above the motor of the Bf 109 E.

Right: Protection against low-level attack: one of several machine-gun positions around one of JG 2's airfields in France. Note the MG 15 machine-gun on an improvised mount.

Wick's ride on the white horse Cribuja was interrupted by saddle problems, but his comrades, including Franz Fiby (2nd from left), were standing by to help.

An armorer installing an ammunition drum for one of the aircraft's MG FF 20-mm cannon. Each drum held just sixty rounds of ammunition. Pilots were therefore urged to only employ the cannon for short, accurate bursts.

The fighters of JG 2 began patrolling again, mainly over the coast, guarding the newly-won territory. They were soon called into action again, however, for British Prime Minister Winston Churchill had no intention of responding to Hitler's offer of a cease-fire or peace treaty.

The first combat near the British coast—which was still officially forbidden—took place on 17 July. *Leutnant* Wick and *Leutnant* Fiby took off from Octeville, near Le Havre, to intercept an English reconnaissance aircraft. They failed to locate the Blenheim, but quite unexpectedly they ran into a squadron of Spitfires. Wick shot down the aircraft at the end of the formation, the so-called "Tail End Charlie," without the rest of the formation realizing it. It was his 15th victory. Wick's air fighting tactic had proved itself: as soon as he spotted enemy aircraft—usually from far away, thanks to his outstanding eyesight—he applied full throttle and placed himself in a favorable position from which to attack. He closed quickly and tried to shoot down his opponent with an accurate burst on the first pass. Then he dove away and withdrew to reassess the situation—exactly as he had been taught by his mentor, Werner Mölders. Wick's habit of flying constantly at full power when in contact with the enemy of course resulted in severe engine wear. Once, without his knowledge, Wick's mechanic carried out a complete engine change during the night. Wick always spoke of his "Black Men" with the highest respect. The ground crews always felt that the victories achieved by their pilots were their own. After all, it was because of their efforts that the Messerschmitts were kept serviceable and ready to fight.

From Beaumont-le-Roger the fighters flew to front-line bases; mainly to Querqueville (west), Theville (Maupertus, east of Cherbourg), or Octeville, near Le Havre. From there they took off on missions over the Channel. Approximately 100 kilometers of water separated France from Great Britain at that point.

The German airmen had to become used to flying over the sea. Regulations required them to wear life vests, which made the already confined cockpit of the Bf 109 seem even more cramped. In addition to the life vest, pilots were equipped with a flare pistol, inflatable life raft, and dye packet. Worn on the upper thigh, the dye packet operated automatically, producing a large green patch on the surface of the water. Concerning over-water operations, Franz Fiby noted:

"...but in time one became accustomed to flying over water. The first time I flew about 20 km off the

Makeshift firing stand for aligning the guns of a Messerschmitt Bf 109 E.

Above: ***Leutnant*** **Wick's first "Yellow 2," a Bf 109 E-3. As a result of carelessness on the part of the ground crew, the aircraft rolled down a hill as it was being parked. As may be seen, the aircraft already wore a modified camouflage finish at the time of the incident (June 1940). The pale blue sides of the fuselage were overpainted with dark green speckles.**

Center: ***Leutnant*** **Fiby and** ***Leutnant*** **Wick.**

Below: Bf 109 E-3s and E-4s of 1./JG 2 in France. In the background on the right is a Bf 108 used as a communications aircraft.

coast I felt a slight uneasiness in spite of my life vest. One began listening attentively to the engine and immediately questioning everything. On leaving the coast, one listened closely and observed the regular vibration of the seat bottom. If everything was running smoothly, then one carried on and watched intently until a coastline with white cliffs finally appeared out of the blue. It might be enemy territory, but at least it was dry. When our time was up we always made our way home quickly, for no one had any desire to fight over the sea in a kite running low on fuel. Later in the evening we flew home from our hideouts. By then full of high spirits, we roared low over railway embankments and scattered grazing cows. Like rascals released from jail, we raced toward 'home.' Those are actions that the honest man never experiences."

On 21 July, just promoted to *Oberleutnant*, Helmut Wick was named *Staffelkapitän* of the *3. Staffel*. Henning Strümpell, who had been promoted to *Major*, assumed command of I./JG 2 in place of *Hauptmann* Roth.

In August the *Luftwaffe* command ordered an intensification of the air war against England. *Leutnant* Fiby wrote:

"By then we had flown over the big brook to England many times, and we knew the south coast of the 'invincible' island very well. On 11 August the war again began taking on a more serious form. I had to miss several missions, as my machine had developed an engine problem. On 11 August the *Staffel* recorded five victories, the *Geschwader* 22, against five losses. It was even broadcast on the radio. Helmut W. got three Tommies, a Curtiss P 36, a Spitfire, and a Hurricane. The air battle over Portland was the biggest our pilots had ever experienced, even the veterans of Spain. There were 120 Me 109s alone, plus the heavy fighters and bombers as bait. The sky was full of English aircraft, and the fight was certainly very difficult. A reporter wrote in the Racial Observer: 'The English fighter squadrons all ran away as soon as a Messerschmitt appeared in the sky.' This sly fox should have tried sitting in an Me so he could see for himself that they

Chateau Beaumont-le-Roger. After the end of the campaign in France the castle became home to part of JG 2. Its owners remained for a while until their activities on behalf of the resistance became too risky. The imposing structure was leveled by American bombers in 1943.

Above: The luxuriously-appointed residence of the American painter Aston Knight, which in late June 1940 became home to the 3. *Staffel*. Knight fled west several days before the arrival of the Germans. Helmut Wick occupied a room on the first floor. Below: Put on a record: to the sound of sweet music, *Gefreiter* Richey, *Leutnant* Fiby and *Unteroffiziere* Tilly and Seeger (from left to right) make themselves comfortable in the garden.

Left: The *3. Staffel* also gladly made use of Knight's rather antiquated swimming pool.

Center: Bf 109s of the *3. Staffel* of JG 2 on patrol over Normandy in June-July 1940.

Below: *Leutnant* Franz Fiby in his "Yellow 14."

Oberfeldwebel Franz Jaenisch in his 109. His personal emblem may be seen beneath the cockpit. The "Mickey Mouse" emblem recalled his service with the Legion Condor in Spain.

Leutnant Wick in "Yellow 1." His new "Yellow 2" was perhaps unserviceable or had yet to be delivered.

Wick in the cockpit of his new "Yellow 2."

Wick's 109 wearing camouflage netting and a tarpaulin over the engine.

German flying boots. Note the map stuck in the top of the right boot and the bandolier of flare cartridges strapped around the pilot's left leg.

Opposite: ***Leutnant*** **Wick in front of his new Bf 109 E-4 "Yellow 2". On the engine cowling is the Horrido pennant, the emblem of JG 2's 3.** ***Staffel.***

Right: The instrument panel of a Messerschmitt Bf 109 E.

The airfield at Querqueville, west of Cherbourg. Situated right on the Channel coast, it was one of the airfields used by JG 2, JG 27 and JG 53 in missions over England.

The newly-promoted *Oberleutnant* Wick.

Boulton Paul Defiant two-seat fighters of No. 264 Squadron. This cumbersome fighter's entire armament was housed in a revolving turret. These machines suffered heavy losses, especially against Bf 109s, and at the end of August they were withdrawn from daylight operations. The Defiant later served as a night-fighter.

The Junkers Ju 87 suffered a similar fate. Without adequate fighter protection the Stukas were almost helpless against Hurricanes and Spitfires.

A Bf 110 C of the 4. *Staffel* of *Zerstörergeschwader* 76. Though fast and heavily armed, the Bf 110 suffered heavy losses at the hands of British fighters.

Chain Home radar station near Dover. In the summer of 1940 the British became the first to use radar technology to detect enemy aircraft. This photograph was taken from the French coast using a special camera. These large stations were supplemented by smaller Chain Home Low sites, which specialized in the detection of low-flying aircraft. The German command underestimated the value of the British radars for a long time.

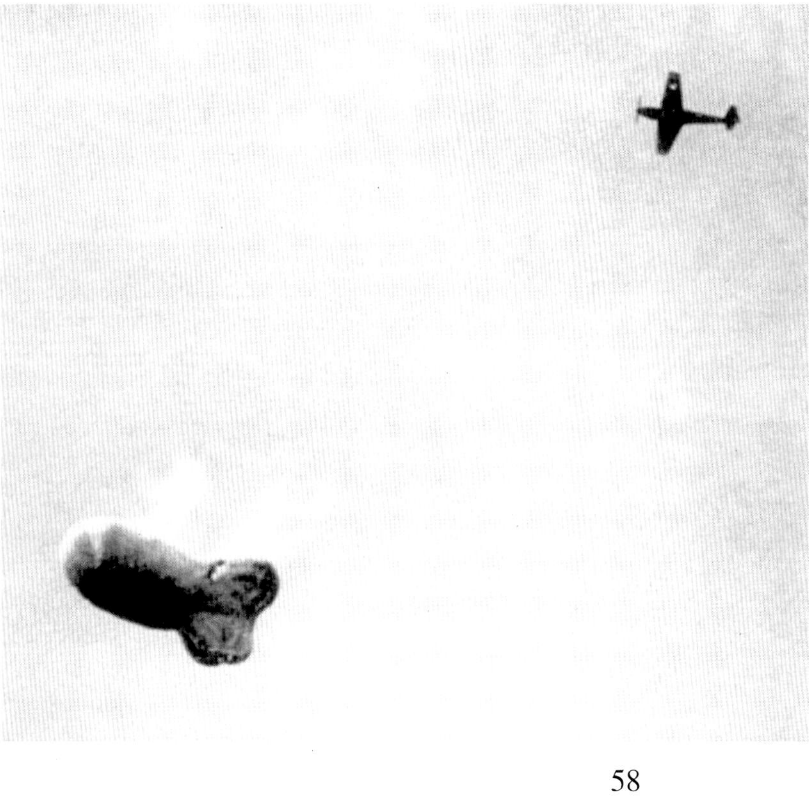

British barrage balloons, with steel cables suspended beneath them, posed a threat to low-flying aircraft. They were easy prey for German fighter pilots. The *3. Staffel* shot up a number of these balloons on 18 August. Franz Fiby wrote: "Countless barrage balloons at 1500 meters. The *Staffel* shot down six."

Two Hurricanes of No. 501 Squadron scramble from Rochford on 15 August. Both were shot down three days later.

didn't run away. This type of reporting had a negative rather than a positive effect, for on reading it the civilian at home said: 'Well then, if the Tommies all run away, it's an easy fight, no danger at all.' These smart alecks should have been forced to dangle their white asses over the water for an hour and a half, seeing nothing but water and enemy territory. One bullet in the radiator was enough for one to voluntarily become a prisoner of war or end up in the drink."

Wick described his mission on 11 August to a war correspondent:

"A squadron of Spitfires dove on us from above and behind. I immediately broke into them. As I came about, I saw a Spitfire behind a 109 and higher up the same thing. The two German fighters did the only correct thing and dove away. The two Spitfires also disappeared. The rest had descended through cloud. But that was only the prelude. What followed happened much faster than I am capable of relating. It was an incredible dogfight. Wherever I looked, aircraft and more aircraft, but the hostiles were easily in the majority. Flying in close formation, three English machines with radial engines came toward me. I pulled the stick into my stomach and got behind the three. A quick look back, no one to interfere for the next few seconds. I moved closer and got the flight leader in my sights. I pressed the buttons and he went down. I pulled up again. Something was happening on my right. I couldn't believe my eyes—the sky was full of Spitfires, all chasing a few poor Messerschmitts. I had no choice but to dive into the beehive and get our fellows out! A Spitfire got on my tail. I dove away at full throttle. Another Spitfire in front of me, and behind? Damn it! Another one was on my tail and I had to dive quickly. I climbed up again. White lines suddenly appeared beside the canopy glass on my right, then more. A quick look to the right, and there was another one behind me and bursts of tracers, or corpse fingers, as we call them, flashed about my ears. I looked behind and left. Good heavens! Three Spitfires on my left! I was surrounded. Under continuous fire, I made a full-power climbing turn to the left. Tracer whizzed past on my left and right and above me. I promised to thank all the gods if my mother's son got out of this mess. Climbing gained me a little breathing space. My few comrades continued to grapple with the numerically superior enemy. Every time I tried to intervene, Spitfires got behind and forced me to break away. A 109 raced past me with a Spitfire on its tail. You're mine, slippery friend! I maneuvered behind the Tommy, got him in my sights, and after a few bursts he fell away. I had a little breathing space, which allowed me to watch the Englishman. He crashed into the water, and even from above I could see that there was a great splash. Afterwards there was nothing left to show that a brave flier had died a hero's death there."

The Messerschmitt's limited range meant that the German fighter pilots had to withdraw after a brief period of combat. *Oberleutnant* Wick scored another victory on the way home, shooting down one of a flight of unsuspecting Hurricanes. It was his 17th victory and his 13th combat.

At Beaumont-le-Roger, Franz Fiby carved three new chevrons in Wick's victory stick. The stick, actually a normal walking stick, had been given to Wick by his *3. Staffel* comrades following his first victory. Franz Fiby had taken on the task of recording Wick's victories on the stick. Each chevron stood for one victory. The type and date were carved beside the chevrons, and soon there would be the Knight's Cross as well.

The Knight's Cross

The fighting in the air grew increasingly difficult. Enemy aircraft were shot down, but some of one's own comrades also failed to return. By now most of the young pilots had become accustomed to death. It was a constant companion, and could claim anyone at any time. On 27 August Franz Fiby wrote in his diary:

"About three weeks ago we flew to Le Havre. Our *Staffel* had already landed, when a Bristol Blenheim serenely emerged from the clouds. The *Stabsschwarm* had its undercarriage down and was about to land. Suddenly, the Blenheim was sighted, gear up, and away. Two minutes later the adjutant sent the enemy kite into the port's main street. Soon afterward a bomb exploded, and a pillar of smoke rose 200 meters into the air. The funniest thing about it was: we on the ground all saw Paul Temme shoot down the enemy plane, but afterwards the flak batteries claimed the kill. None of the crew survived, as the kite was flying too low for them to bail out. The pilot had his papers and date book on him. He was a Pilot Officer, 21 years and two days old. His notes revealed that he had often bombed Cherbourg by night. His mother had probably already received his last letter. He looked very charming in his photo. As we looked at his papers everyone thought the same thing: pity, he was surely a fine chap, and half an hour from now the same thing might happen to me. That's just how war is. Unfortunately, this was Paul's last victory. Several days later he failed to return. He was seen over there with radiator damage, and the others were quite certain that he made a forced landing on the island or bailed out."

Announcement by the Armed Forces High Command: 26 August 1940: in yesterday's air battles the Richthofen Geschwader surpassed 250 victories. Oberleutnant Wick scored his 19th and 20th victories.

Wick's "Yellow 2," Werknr. 5344, photographed at Beaumont-le-Roger.

Above: The aircraft of *Geschwader* adjutant Paul Temme, who was forced down in England on 18 August and became a prisoner of war.

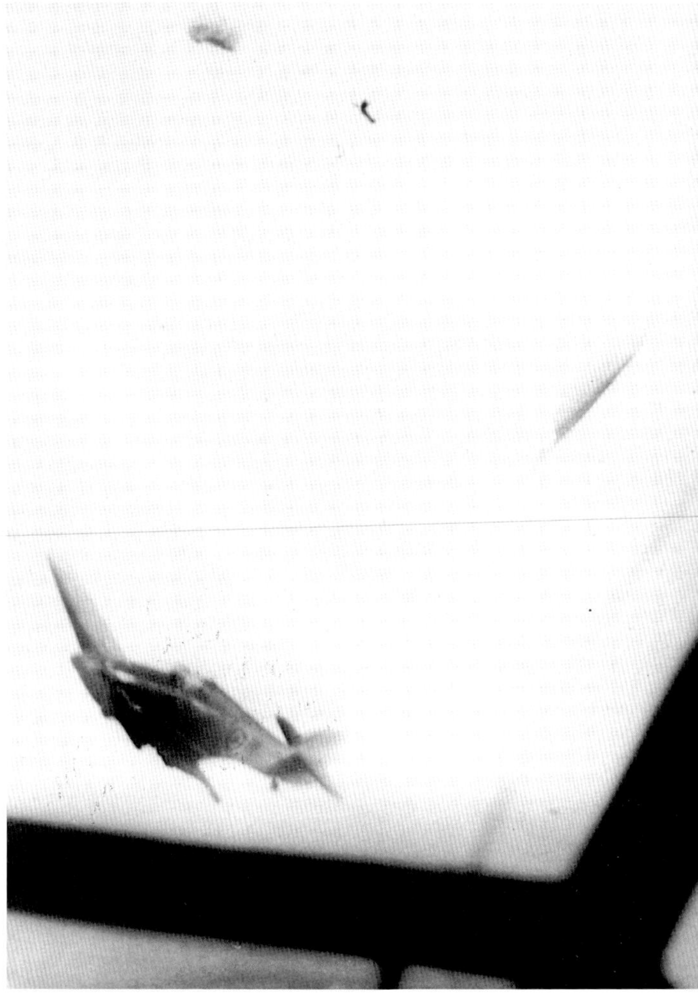

Center: A Hurricane loses a wing after colliding with a Do 17 (the wing is just visible on the right of the photo). The Hurricane's pilot, Flying Officer Higgs, was killed.

Below: This photo was taken by the gun camera of a Spitfire flown by Pilot Officer David Crook of No. 69 Squadron as he shot down a Bf 109 E of JG 2.

Wick's Bf 109 with 22 victory bars on its rudder.

Another look at the map. To the left of Wick is *Feldwebel* Stritzel.

When this bulletin came over the airwaves Wick was with his comrades. With a wink, he declared:

"Gentlemen, you have been misinformed. That's old news. This afternoon I shot down my 21st and 22nd."

Everyone knew that 20 victories meant the Knight's Cross. This much desired decoration for merit and bravery had been created on 1 September 1939 as a further grade of the Iron Cross.* Those who wore it were highly respected. And now Wick had surpassed the magic number. Soon the press, in the form of war correspondents, came calling. *Leutnant* Wick was interviewed extensively about his life and his victories. An interview was recorded for the radio. Somewhat shy and reserved at first, he soon came to enjoy being the center of attention, vividly describing his actions for the reporters. Of course a whole series of photographs was taken.

On 27 August *Oberleutnant* Wick received the Knight's Cross from *Reichsmarschall* Hermann Göring's hand. He thus became the second member of JG 2 *"Richthofen"* to receive the decoration, after *Oberstleutnant* Bühlow. Göring had invited the young *Oberleutnant* to Karinhall, his country estate, to present him the decoration in person. Wick took advantage of this audience with Göring to request the Iron Cross, First Class for his faithful wingman, Franz Fiby. The

*For more on the Knight's Cross of the Iron Cross and other German decorations see: *Kurt-G. Klietmann: Auszeichnungen des Deutschen Reiches 1936-1945.* Motorbuch Verlag, Stuttgart 1996 (6th Edition).

A war correspondent interviews soon-to-be Knight's Cross wearer *Oberleutnant* Wick about his missions for a radio broadcast.

Left: *Oberleutnant* Wick uses his hands to describe an air combat for the benefit of a war correspondent. The original caption: "After returning from combat over England, on a Channel Coast airfield an *Oberleutnant* describes the details of his latest victory for a war correspondent."

Below: Photograph for the press. Wick and the pilots of the *3. Staffel* by the tail of his 109. Left of him is *Leutnant* Kurt Votel, right *Leutnant* Franz Fiby.

Photo portrait of Ursel and Helmut Wick after the awarding of the Knight's Cross by *Reichsmarschall* Göring, who also ordered Wick to take four days leave.

Ursel, little Walter and Helmut Wick in the garden of the parent's home in Berlin-Wannsee.

request was granted. At *Karinhall* Wick met Frau Emmy Göring and her young daughter, Edda. Finally, Göring gave Wick four days special leave. Helmut went to Berlin and paid a surprise visit to his parents, and of course Ursel and little Walter. As much as he enjoyed spending time with his family again, part of Helmut's heart was always with his men in France. He was absent from missions over the Channel at a time when things there were heating up.

Since 28 August the entire *Jagdgeschwader "Richthofen" Nr. 2* had been based at Mardyck and Oye Plage (*III. Gruppe*), between Dunkirk and Calais. This move was the result of planned mass attacks on London. The pilots of JG 2 welcomed the move, as it meant a much shorter flight to England—40 kilometers, or less than half of what they were used to. What was not diminished, however, was the intensity of the fighting, as the British continued to resist stubbornly.

Opposite: Title page of the *Berlin Illustrated News* of 19 September 1940. By the time this issue was printed Wick had added another 10 victories to his total, and had also become *Gruppenkommandeur*.

Nummer 38 19. September 1940

49. Jahrgang Preis 20 Pfennig

Berliner Illustrirte Zeitung

Nach dem 22. Luftsieg

Einer der erfolgreichsten deutschen Jagdflieger, Hauptmann Wick, berichtet von diesem Kampf: [illegible]

Hauptmann and *Gruppenkommandeur*

When Wick returned to the *Geschwader* he found that a handful of his comrades were closing in on his total, including *Oberfeldwebel* Machold, with 20 enemy aircraft shot down. There had been heavy fighting in recent days. *Oberleutnant* Wick did not waste time, however. On 4 September he resumed his successful ways by downing two Hurricanes over Kent.

To his great surprise, Wick received an early promotion to *Hauptmann* and, as part of the *Luftwaffe*'s program of injecting youth into command positions, on 9 September he was officially named *Kommandeur* of the *I. Gruppe* of JG 2. Wick could scarcely comprehend it all. He had only recently been promoted early to *Oberleutnant*, then *Staffelkapitän*, then the Knight's Cross from Göring, the radio, the press, and now *Hauptmann* and *Gruppenkommandeur*!

The *Luftwaffe*'s large-scale raids on London began on 7 September. Wick's *Gruppe* took part in these attacks. He claimed Spitfires on 5 and 6 September, and his hunter's luck held true on the 7th, 8th, and 9th. After 10 September the *Richthofen Geschwader* scaled back its activities. On the 15th of the month the unit

4 September 1940. Morning on Mardyck airfield in Belgium, where the *I.* and *II. Gruppe* of JG 2 had been based since 28 August.

Helmut Wick back from his first combat mission after returning from Berlin. The stress of the action is still visible in his face.

An English fighter pilot in his Spitfire.

Above: The Luftwaffe's bombing campaign against London began on 7 September. Hermann Göring, Bruno Loerzer, Hans Jeschonnek and other senior air force officers watch from the French coast as German fighters and bombers pass overhead on their way to London. Below: Dornier Do 17 Z bombers of *Kampfgeschwader* 2 en route to England.

Messerschmitt Bf 109s fly escort for Do 17 bombers.

A Heinkel He 111 over England.

St. Peter's Square in the heart of London. In the background is St. Paul's Cathedral. Many English cities were heavily damaged by German bombing, even if they did not suffer as badly as German and Japanese cities later in the war. The German attacks also proved a serious tactical error. The German leadership expected the bombing to crush the will of the English people, but they were wrong. The attacks had exactly the opposite effect, as was the case in Germany later in the war. The Luftwaffe's change in tactics took the pressure off RAF Fighter Command, whose bases had previously been the main targets.

"Achtung Spitfire!" The elegant yet lethal British fighter was the Luftwaffe's most dangerous foe in the fighting over the Channel and Great Britain.

Wick's stained and dirty "Yellow 2" at Mardyck shortly before the "2" was replaced by the double chevrons of a *Gruppen-kommandeur*. The engine cowling has been painted—probably white—to better allow pilots to distinguish friend from foe in the air. The sword and the lettering in the Horrido emblem appear rather dark, which may have something to do with the type of film used.

A comrade pins the second star, representing the rank of *Hauptmann*, on Helmut Wick's shoulder board. On the far left is *Hauptmann* Greisert, who assumed temporary command of JG 2 after Wick's failure to return pending the arrival of *Hauptmann* Balthasar.

Mission briefing.

Major Strümpell and *Hauptmann* Wick, obviously in high spirits.

Opposite: Back in Beaumont-le-Roger, now as *Hauptmann* and *Kommandeur* of *I. Gruppe* of JG 2.

Wick's 109 with four more victory bars on the rudder. Behind it are two mechanics.

***Hauptmann* Wick with *Major* Wolfgang Schellmann, *Kommodore* of JG 2 "Richthofen" since early September 1940.**

***Hauptmann* Wick's 109, once again *Werknummer* 5344, which he also flew as *Kommandeur* of I./JG 2. Although no longer a member of the 3. *Staffel*, Wick left the Horrido emblem on his aircraft. In the background an aircraft of Stab/JG 53.**

moved back to Normandy. A number of its aircraft were in need of a complete overhaul.

Wick was popular with most of his men regardless of rank, for he thought and acted like a practical man, rather than a stiff-necked Prussian:

"He was a very comfortable superior," recalled Günter Seeger, then an *Unteroffizier* in the *3. Staffel*. *"We pilots all got along well with Wick."*

Feldmarschall Hugo Sperrle was a grim, imposing figure, little loved by many of the troops. After inspecting the *I. Gruppe*, he berated Wick for the sloppy appearance of the ground personnel. Wick countered, and said to the hefty senior officer:

"Herr Feldmarschall, these men work from morning till night, they work like crazy to keep our machines serviceable, don't you think that's more important than a damned haircut or a clean uniform?"

Sperrle's monocle dropped from his eye. He said nothing.

Despite his popularity, Wick still had his critics. He tended to behave rather recklessly on operations. As soon as he sighted an enemy aircraft he rammed the throttle full open and charged after the enemy without worrying whether his men could keep up. Günter Seeger:

"Wick was always a role model for us pilots. He was a good flier and had outstanding eyesight, which were great advantages in air combat. As a *Kommandeur* or *Kommodore* he was perhaps too quick in the air, sometimes causing the *Gruppe* or *Geschwader* to become strung out behind him."

Many were inspired to do the same as Wick, but not everyone was willing to take the same risks. Wick's victories were a result of his daredevil nature, combined with a cook head and brilliant eyesight. He

Left: *Unteroffizier* Günter Seeger.

Another photo of Wick's machine during his time as *Gruppenkommandeur*.

amassed victories with enormous enthusiasm. Wick definitely wanted to become number one among German fighter pilots.

On 5 October, while flying escort for Ju 88 bombers, Wick shot down three Hurricanes over Southampton, victories 37, 38, and 39. His 40th fell during a late afternoon mission. Helmut Wick:

"Toward evening we flew another mission. For the first time since my beginner's period I was careless. But I had just shot down my 39th and was eager to make it 40. What I did next was pure rubbish. I attacked a squadron of Spitfires, which had already spotted us, from an unfavorable position. The one I attacked wouldn't go down; instead he dove away. Furious, I gave chase, but the rest of the Spitfires got behind me. The wild pursuit went from several thousand meters down to 500 meters. The English flying behind me were inferior in speed and lost me in the clouds, while I closed the distance on my victim. I fired and he went down. As he fluttered down, I climbed back up and saw that three of the pursuing Spitfires had found me again. I turned into them and shot down the one on the right; however, this placed me in a disadvantageous position relative to the other two. Fortunately they broke the other way, otherwise things could have become very uncomfortable for me."

Hauptmann Wick was well on his way to overtaking his two closest rivals for the scoring lead, *Major* Adolf Galland and *Oberstleutnant* Werner Mölders. Now he was stealing the show. There were many who found it amusing to watch the "Victory Race" between the two highly-decorated veterans of Spain and the short, ambitious Wick, who had only been an *Oberleutnant* for a few weeks. It seemed obvious who would become the new number one in the not too distant future. While Wick never lost his respect for his old mentor Mölders, he was unable to begin any sort of relationship with Galland.

In the summer of 1940 Werner Mölders (right), *Kommodore* of JG 51, was the leading German fighter ace. On 21 September he became the first fighter pilot to receive the Oak Leaves after his 40th victory. Next to Mölders is *General* Loerzer, on the far right *Reichsmarschall* Göring.

Adolf Galland flew close-support missions in Spain and Poland. Here he is seen as a *Major* and *Kommodore* of JG 26.

There were also strong competitors within the ranks of the *Richthofen Geschwader*. Foremost was *Oberfeldwebel* Werner Machold (center), who was awarded the Knight's Cross on 5 September. He scored 26 victories by the start of November 1940.

Leutnant Siegfried Schnell was awarded the Knight's Cross on 9 November 1940.

Hauptmann Otto Bertram as *Kommandeur* of III./JG 2. After his two brothers, both pilots, were shot down and killed, he was transferred to a training unit.

Oberleutnant Hans "Assi" Hahn was also part of the illustrious circle of Knight's Cross wearers in 1940. He received the decoration on 24 September.

Knight's Cross wearer *Hauptmann* Karl-Heinz Krahl assumed command of the I. *Gruppe* after Wick was promoted.

Flying Officer John Dundas, the ace pilot of No. 609 Squadron.

There were also experts on the other side, such as Flight Lieutenant Robert Stanford Tuck, seen here in the cockpit of his Hurricane while commanding officer of No. 257 Squadron. Wick's score at the end of 1940 was 18 victories.

Berliner Illustrirte Zeitung

Keiner älter als 30 Jahre

Deutschlands beste Jagdflieger

Oberstleutnant Werner Mölders,

[Sohn] eines Reserve-Offiziers aus Gelsenkirchen, der [i]m Weltkrieg fiel, erfolgreichster Jagdflieger der [L]egion „Condor" mit 14 Abschüssen, Träger des [S]panienkreuzes in Gold mit Brillanten, der Medalla [d]e la Campana und Medalla Militar, 1940 Major [d]er Luftwaffe und Kommodore eines Jagdgeschwa[d]ers, nach 20 Abschüssen im Westen der erste Jagd[f]lieger, dem der Führer das Ritterkreuz verlieh — [u]nd dabei erst 27 Jahre alt: Das sind einige Daten [a]us dem Leben eines jungen deutschen Flieger[of]fiziers, der am 25. Oktober 1940 nach seinem [...] Luftsieg vom Führer bevorzugt zum Oberst[-]leutnant befördert wurde.

Major Adolf Galland.

Der 28jährige Offizier ist Kommodore eines Jagdgeschwaders. Seit 1935 Jagdflieger, nahm er a[m] polnischen Feldzug als Staffelkapitän teil und erhielt zwei Wochen nach Kriegsbeginn schon das Eise[rne] Kreuz II. Klasse. Mit 50 Abschüssen führte er Mitte Oktober die Reihe der erfolgreichsten Jagdflieg[er] an. Der Führer verlieh ihm zwei Tage nach Major Mölders das Eichenlaub zum Ritterkreuz.

Hauptmann Helmut Wick — 25 Jahre alt.

April 1936 trat er als Fahnenjunker bei der Luftwaffe ein, wurde 1938 Leutnant, [...] Hauptmann. Im September erhielt er das Ritterkreuz für seinen 20. Luftsieg. [In] den folgenden vier Wochen schoß er weitere 20 Jäger ab und wurde dafür vom Führer mit dem Eichenlaub zum Ritterkreuz ausgezeichnet.

Major Wolfgang Schellmann

ist 29 Jahre alt. Auch er kämpfte als Jagdflieger in der Legion „Condor", kehrte mit deutschen und spanischen Auszeichnungen in die Heimat zurück; er wurde im Juli 1940 außer der Reihe zum Major befördert. Heute führt er ebenfalls als Kommodore ein Jagdgeschwader.

Oberleutnant Hans Hahn — 26 Jahre alt.

Er stammt aus Gotha und wurde 1937 Fluglehrer in einer Jagdfliegerschule, 1938 Stabskompaniefahrer in einem Jagdgeschwader. Er zählt zu den erfolgreichsten Jagdfliegern seiner Luftflotte und wurde am 5. Oktober mit dem Ritterkreuz ausgezeichnet.

Major Günther Lützow.

Der 29jährige Offizier wurde in Kiel geboren. Schon bevor er Soldat wurde, lernte er fliegen. Als Freiwilliger der Legion „Condor" nahm Lützow am spanischen Befreiungskrieg teil, wurde zum Hauptmann befördert und im November 1939 zum Kommandeur einer Jagdgruppe ernannt.

Hauptmann Wilhelm Balthasar — 26 Jahre alt.

Sein Vater fiel als Reserve-Offizier im Weltkrieg vor Lille 1918 als Oberleutnant. Hiltere er mit zwei Kameraden in einen aufsehenerregenden Langstreckenflug rund um Afrika, wobei [...] bei Fh 104" insgesamt [...] Kilometer zurückflogen. Heute ist er Staffelkapitän.

Hauptmann Oesau.

Der Staffelkapi[tän] einer Jagdsta[ffel] hat sich als Ja[gd]flieger im Wes[ten] besonders aus[ge]zeichnet. Auch erhielt bei sein[em] 20. Abschuß v[om] Führer das Rit[ter]kreuz des Eisern[en] Kreuzes verlieh[en].

PK Sporth (Weltbild) [...] Archiv Deutscher V[er]lag (1), PK Ri[...] (Atlantic), PK Sc[...]bert (Atlantic), Weltbild, PK Sto[...] (Weltbild)

One of the many accounts that appeared in German news magazines concerning Germany's most successful fighter pilots. The headline reads, "None older than thirty years – Germany's best fighter pilots."

The Oak Leaves
Audience with the Führer

The fanfares of the *Wehrmacht* communiqué blared from the radio, and once again the name Wick was heard:

Announcement by the Armed Forces High Command: 6 October 1940: Hauptmann Wick shot down five enemy fighters in one day and raised his victory total to 41.

In the late afternoon of 6 October Wick received orders to report to the *Reichsmarschall* in Berlin at 1500 hours the following day. Even though it wasn't stated, it seemed clear what this meant—he had passed the 40 mark, which meant the Oak Leaves. Helmut Wick had thus become the first member of the *Geschwader*, the third of the *Luftwaffe*, and the fourth member of the entire armed forces to be awarded this

Prior to leaving to receive the Oak Leaves—from the left: *Hauptmann* Seegert, *Hauptmann* Wick, *Oberleutnant* Pflanz, *Oberleutnant* Leie.

An enthusiastic Wick describes the shooting down of an enemy aircraft.

Wick proudly displays his victory stick.

Opposite: farewell to his comrades. He certainly won't run short of cigarettes in the next few days. On the left is Rudi Pflanz, who drove all night across Normandy to get Wick to Berlin on time.

This photo does not show Wick waving a handkerchief, as has often been claimed. Instead he is aiming his victory stick at the camera.

high decoration. As the weather was too poor to fly, and the next day was forecast to be no better, that evening Helmut Wick and Rudi Pflanz set off by car.

With iron determination, Rudi Pflanz drove the long distance from Normandy to Berlin. The weather worsened; nevertheless, they made good progress. Every offer by Wick to take the wheel fell on deaf ears. His friend was determined that he should appear before the *Reichsmarschall* the next morning fresh and rested. As the pair roared through a German town at dawn they were stopped by a policeman. Before the man could speak, Wick said to him:

"Do you see the many suitcases in the back seat? Unfortunately we have no room for you."

Perplexed, the officer looked at Wick's Knight's Cross. He said not a word, instead responding with a snappy salute.

Hauptmann Wick checked in at the State Ministry of Aviation at 1500 hours on 7 October, right on time. There, in addition to Hermann Göring, he met *Generalfeldmarschall* Milch, *Generaloberst* Udet, *General* Student, and *General* Bodenschatz. After Wick had lunched with the high-ranking officers, he and Göring left in the *Reichsmarschall*'s special train for Berchtesgaden. It wasn't hard to figure out who was waiting for him there.

The young *Hauptmann* arrived at the Berghof at 1700 hours on 8 September. Wick had to wait for a while, then Hitler received him in the great room. With words of gratitude, the *Führer* presented him with the Oak Leaves. The two men sat down together, and for about a quarter of an hour Wick spoke with the Supreme Commander of the Armed Forces about his experiences. When Hitler learned that Wick planned to visit his family in Berlin, he invited him to travel to the capital with him aboard his special train. Wick was

Opposite: With the *Führer* in Berchtesgaden. After receiving the Oak Leaves from Hitler, Wick was allowed to travel to Berlin in the *Führer*'s special train. During the journey he had the opportunity to speak with Hitler at length. Right: October 13, 1940: Helmut Wick says goodbye to his father in Berlin.

enthusiastic. During the trip to Berlin he had the chance to speak with the *Führer* at length. Among other things, Hitler told him that the invasion of England had already been postponed three times, and that he—like Göring—hoped that air attacks alone might bring England to her knees. As well, efforts were already underway to gain control of the French, and soon also the English colonies. Hitler also spoke of a future conflict with Russia, declaring that the "Bloodhound" Stalin was too headstrong and unpredictable. He also let it be known that Wick was soon to become the *Kommodore* of JG 27.

In Berlin there was a joyous reunion with his family. Son Walter had turned one year old just a few days earlier. In the evening, at the invitation of Reich press chief Dr. Dietrich, Wick gave a talk on the fighting on the Channel for domestic and foreign journalists. The young officer answered their questions in his familiar graphic style. This meeting with the press gave Wick the idea of traveling around Germany, speaking about the war in the air at schools and other institutions.

The next day Helmut visited his mother in the hospital and took lunch with her there. She was in fact his stepmother, but Helmut treated her as if she were his real mother. The press also appeared, and news of his visit soon reached the kitchen, where an excited group of kitchen maids wanted to see the young Knight's Cross wearer. Wick, of course, did them this favor and autographed cards. On his return to the *Geschwader* there was more celebrating. The weather was poor, severely hampering operations.

On 17 October Wick's *Gruppe* was ordered to fly to Brest to escort Stuka dive-bombers and twin-engined fighters attacking a British convoy. Seeing it as a 400-km pleasure flight, the pilots welcomed the mission. The weather had improved, although visibility was still restricted by haze, but the flight from Beaumont-le-Roger to Brest posed no serious navigational problems. The pilots didn't even need a map, and there was no need to wear the bulky life vests. Takeoff was at 1630 hours. The *Gruppe* was soon flying west in loose formation at a height of 1500 meters with Wick in the lead. The Messerschmitt fighters flew serenely through the afternoon sky. There was radio silence; in fact, most hadn't even turned on their radios. Why should they? They weren't expecting to meet English fighters, or to hear the warning call "Achtung Spitfires!" The whole thing was rather like a pleasant Sunday outing. Apparently no one was following their exact course, either. Why should they? After all, the *Kommandeur* was leading. The *Kapitän* of the *2. Staffel*, *Oberleutnant* Bethke, nevertheless had his doubts. He looked at his watch. By his reckoning they should have been in the Mt. Saint Michel area by then, or at least have flown

Above: Wick in Berlin-Wannsee, where his parents lived. Opposite: One of the many press reports on the awarding of the Oak Leaves.

Major Helmuth Wick erhielt das Eichenlaub zum Ritterkreuz des Eisernen Kreuzes. Helmuth Wick, einer der erfolgreichsten Jagdflieger, wurde vom Führer das Eichenlaub zum Ritterkreuz des Eisernen Kreuzes verliehen. Gleichzeitig wurde er zum Major befördert, nachdem er erst am 4. 9. 40 zum Hauptmann ernannt worden war.

Major Helmuth Wick was decorated with the Oak Leaf to the Knight Cross of the Iron Cross. Helmuth Wick, one of the most successful German fighters, was also promoted as Major, after being appointed captain on the 4. 9. 40.
PK-Ritter-Pressebildzentrale

IM NAMEN
DES DEUTSCHEN VOLKES

VERLEIHE ICH

DEM MAJOR

HELMUT WICK

DAS EICHENLAUB
ZUM RITTERKREUZ
DES EISERNEN KREUZES

FÜHRERHAUPTQUARTIER
DEN 25. OKTOBER 1940

DER FÜHRER
UND OBERSTE BEFEHLSHABER
DER WEHRMACHT

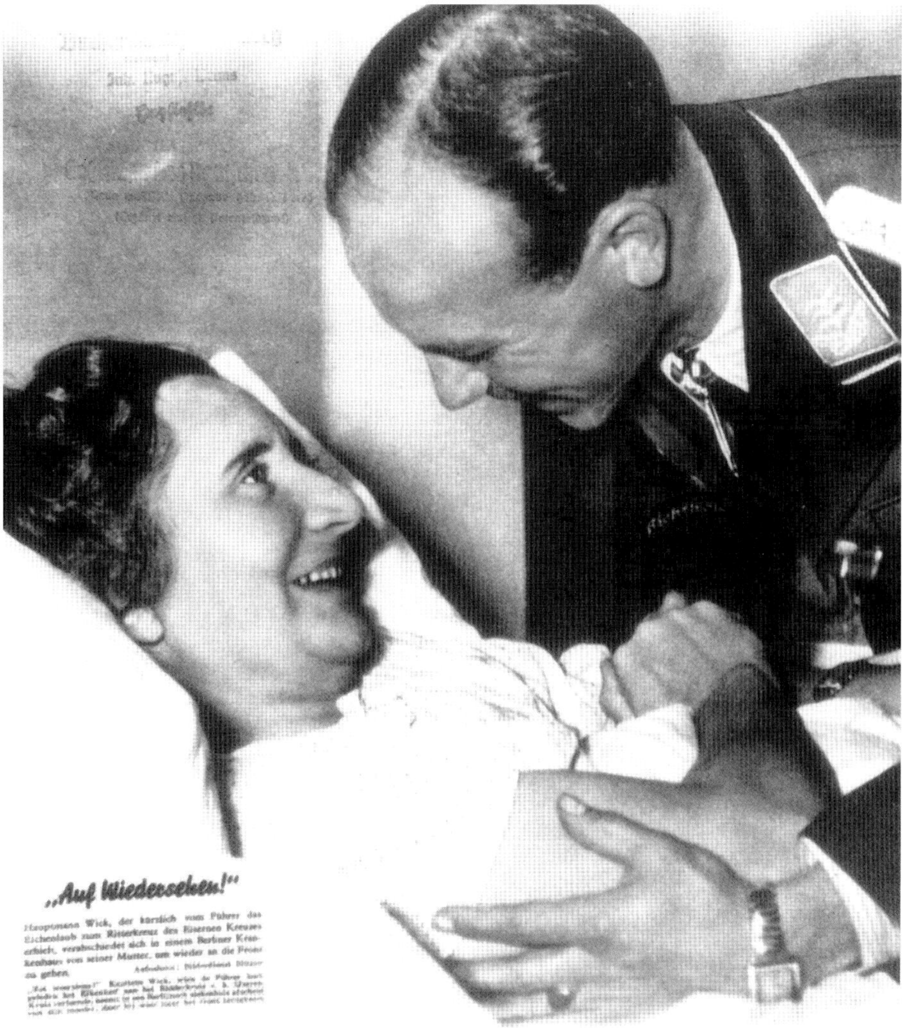

The proud wearer of the Oak Leaves visits his mother-in-law in a Berlin hospital.

Opposite: Award document for the Knight's Cross of the Iron Cross with Oak Leaves.

Wick in conversation with one of the "Black Men" of the ground personnel.

The fighter ace signs an autograph for mountain troops visiting the *Richthofen Geschwader*.

Wick's 109, with open cowling for engine servicing.

This page and following: These photographs were probably taken in the afternoon on 17 October 1940, shortly before the eventful flight to Brest. Note the supplementary armor glass panel which has been installed in front of the windscreen.

over the west coast of the Cotentin Peninsula. Perhaps Wick was flying farther south on purpose. The area over which they found themselves lacked any significant landmarks. Then a city appeared in the mist beneath them. While Bethke was trying to locate the city on his map, the *Kommandeur* made a slight course correction to the left. There was no water to be seen anywhere. Suddenly it dawned on Bethke: according to his map, the city had to be Rennes. That meant that they were far south of course heading, for the west coast of Brittany. But what difference did it make? It was just an extra 100 kilometers. Apparently Wick was turning the transfer flight into an excursion over an area where they had never flown before—that crazy Wick! The water must appear soon. Then a blue strip appeared, and *Oberleutnant* Bethke waited for a turn to the northwest in the direction of Brest. But Wick gave no indication of changing course. About an hour had passed since the city. The *Gruppe* bravely followed their leader out over the water. There was an island, which must be Belle Ille. But Wick flew past it. Bethke deliberated. He thought and thought, but was unable to completely explain what was happening. Perhaps Wick had a secret mission. And if he didn't—if he believed we were flying over Jersey in the direction of Brest? Even a wearer of the Oak Leaves was just a man. Siegfried Bethke thought about the humiliation he would face if he was wrong after all. But then he became certain that the *Gruppe* was flying toward the open sea and would soon pass the point where it would be too late to return to the mainland. Without life vests they would die pitifully in the water of the Bay of Biscay—the entire *I. Gruppe*. Bethke radioed his commanding officer—nothing. None of the pilots had his radio switched on. Without hesitating, he flew up to the *Kommandeur*'s machine, waggled his wings, and then began a 180-degree turn. The others began to turn, as well. They reached the mainland, and flew along the coast toward the northwest. The matter wasn't over, however, for they no longer had enough fuel to reach Brest. Airfields were scarce, and many were rendered unusable by the French at the last minute. The terrain

***Oberleutnant* Siegfried Bethke. His alertness during the flight of 17 October saved the lives of more than 20 pilots of the I. *Gruppe*.**

was rocky, and a wheels-up landing on the beach seemed to make the most sense. But luck was with them, for a seemingly intact airfield suddenly appeared before them. All of the *Gruppe*'s aircraft landed safely on their last drops of fuel. Wick, who seemed lost in thought, thanked Bethge. He admitted that he was not properly orientated and had no map in his aircraft. He failed to pay attention to the time, and really believed that he was on course. His thoughts were probably elsewhere—his visit with the *Führer*, the promotion to *Kommodore*, the victory race with Mölders and Galland. He subsequently remarked, *"That could very easily have gone wrong!"*

In the evening the young pilots celebrated their deliverance. Few of them gave the incident much thought; after all, for the past few months they had faced death on an almost daily basis in the form of a Hurricane or Spitfire and had become inured to the danger. The mission planned for the next day was called off because of a bad storm. And so the aircraft of the *I. Gruppe* returned in pairs to Beaumont-le-Roger. A heavy buildup of cloud resulted in a number of forced landings. *Fähnrich* Siepold was killed in a crash, and *Unteroffizier* Gellert suffered serious injuries.

Youngest *Major* and *Kommodore* in the *Luftwaffe*

On 19 October Helmut Wick was officially promoted to *Major* and named *Kommodore* of JG 27. Wick's enthusiasm was subdued, however, for he had no desire to leave his *Gruppe*. After much thought, he asked the *Reichsmarschall* not to appoint him *Kommodore* of JG 27, and instead leave him remaining with his *Gruppe*. The next day, to his great surprise, *Major* Wick was named *Kommodore* of *JG "Richthofen" Nr. 2*. The 25-year-old thus became the youngest *Major* and *Geschwaderkommodore* in the *Luftwaffe*. *Major* Schellmann, who had commanded JG 2 since the beginning of September, was placed in command of JG 27.

Many criticized this appointment—entrusting a 25-year-old with command of a *Geschwader*, a unit with a personnel strength of 2,300 men. But the *Luftwaffe* command's policy of placing young combat pilots in command of *Geschwader* made it possible.

Being *Kommodore* of course meant more work, including bureaucratic paperwork, which Wick hated. Sometimes he wished that he could be a simple *Oberleutnant* and *Staffelkapitän* again.

A member of the ground crew removes camouflage from the tail of Wick's aircraft.

Above: A look into the muzzle of a 20-mm MG FF cannon.

Opposite: the youngest *Major* in the Luftwaffe.

Left: Wick in conversation with a mechanic, who is possibly explaining required maintenance work or some modification.

Opposite: Helmut Wick in his element. The tactical symbol of a *Kommodore* has yet to be painted on his 109. Wick's personal emblem, the little bird, is visible beneath and behind the cockpit.

Above and left: Final preparations for takeoff.

The new *Kommodore* of the *Richthofen Geschwader* signing autographs in his office.

Wick with a member of the headquarters staff at the castle.

Geschwader order issued by *Major* Wick after assuming command as *Kommodore*. "The *Reichsmarschall* has bestowed upon me a great honor by naming me the *Kommodore* of the famous *Jagdgeschwader Richthofen Nr. 2*. I have assumed command of the *Geschwader* as of today. I wish to express my thanks to my predecessor *Major* Schellmann, who in exemplary fashion maintained the traditions of the *Richthofen Geschwader* and added to its fame. I am thoroughly aware of this weighty responsibility and am determined to lead the *Geschwader* in the same spirit of absolute readiness for action that it has always shown. I want to be your leader by example, but also your best comrade. In this sense let us continue forward from victory to victory until the final triumph."

JAGDGESCHWADER RICHTHOFEN Nr.2 Gefechtsstand,24.10.40.

G e s c h w a d e r b e f e h l .

Der Herr Reichsmarschall hat mir die hohe Ehre erwiesen, mich als Kommodore an die Spitze des ruhmreichen Jagdgeschwaders Richthofen Nr.2 zu berufen. Ich habe mit dem heutigen Tage die Führung des Geschwaders übernommen. Mein besonderer Dank gilt meinem Vorgänger Major Schellmann, der es in vorbildlicher Weise verstanden hat, die Tradition des Richthofen - Geschwaders zu wahren und seinen Ruhm zu mehren.

Ich bin mir der großen verpflichtenden Verantwortung durchaus bewußt und bin gewillt, in dem bisherigen Geiste der restlosen Einsatzbereitschaft Aller, das Geschwader zu führen. Ich will Euer Führer im Sinne des Vorlebens und Vorleistens, zugleich aber Euer bester Kamerad sein. In diesem Sinne weiterhin vorwärts von Sieg zu Sieg, bis zum Endsiege.

Obergefreiter Dahl working on a portrait of the new *Kommodore* at the end of October.

Göring's visit to Querqueville in October 1940.

Above: An *Unteroffizier* reports. From left: Stolle, Wick, and Göring; on the far right is Jeschonnek.

Right: Pilot Bruno Stolle at attention before the *Reichsmarschall*. In the left background Helmut Wick.

The entire party moves on to continue the inspection and talk further.

Opposite: Helmut Wick in conversation with Hermann Göring and Hans Jeschonnek (center), the *Luftwaffe* Chief of Staff. Above: A Bristol Blenheim light bomber and night-fighter of the RAF. Unfortunately for its crews, RAF fighter pilots occasionally mistook this aircraft for the German Ju 88.

The RAF's fighters continued to fight. Here Hurricanes of No. 601 (County of London) Squadron on patrol.

The gun camera of a Messerschmitt Bf 109 captures a Hurricane's final moments. Such photographs are rare, for cameras were seldom installed in German fighters at that time.

Few missions were flown during the rest of October on account of bad weather. The last month's missions had left visible scars on the pilots and had created many gaps in the *Geschwader*. Many had been killed, wounded, or taken prisoner. The others were showing signs of stress, Wick among them. He smoked heavily and drank a lot of black coffee.

At the beginning of November there were increased opportunities for combat and victories. Wick shot down three of the enemy on 5 November. The next day, 6 November, he surpassed this feat by claiming five victories. But his nerves seemed to be stretched to the limit, as he himself openly admitted:

"I can't say exactly what was wrong with me on that 6 November, whether I wasn't at my best, or my nerves were no longer able to keep up. When I had shot down my second Englishman I just wanted to go home. I'm sure I had enough fuel for a few more minutes, but the urge to fly home was suddenly overpowering. If, however, I might come to my own defense, there wasn't much I could have done with the few extra minutes if I had needed it. When he had completed our 180-degree turn and set course for home, I in fact saw three Spitfires below me. They were obviously heading back from over the sea. I was first to spot them, and I moved in quickly and knocked the first one down. But then I said to myself: down with these fellows! If I let these two Englishmen get away, tomorrow they might shoot down one of my men. So away with them—I clenched my teeth and began the next attack."

Wick downed both of the enemy fighters. Worn out and completely done in, after landing he fell into the arms of his very best comrade.

On 4 November the *Richthofen Geschwader* was expecting more high-ranking visitors—Göring, Sperrle, and other officers of the *Luftwaffe* general staff. Wick assembled the entire *Geschwader*. *Reichsmarschall* Göring spoke to the men about new operational possibilities and lauded Wick's accomplishments. Then the non-flying personnel were dismissed, and Göring questioned the pilots about the number of missions they had flown and the victories they had claimed. He also bestowed a number of promotions.

A Spitfire down on the French coast, autumn 1940.

Above and below: Bad weather—these photographs were probably taken near Le Havre.

Completely exhausted after returning from the combat mission on 6 November, when Wick scored his 52nd victory.

On 5 November there was a meeting of various commanders of fighter and bomber units. Mölders (commander of JG 51) attended, as did Galland, leader of JG 26. On this occasion Hermann Göring presented the young commander of the *Richthofen Geschwader* with a large gold ring bearing the emblem of the *Luftwaffe*.

Announcement by the Armed Forces High Command: 16 November 1940: under the command of Major Wick the Baron von Richthofen Fighter Wing achieved its 500th aerial victory.

To mark the 500th victory by the *Richthofen Geschwader*, on 22 November—exactly one year after JG 2's first victory—the *Kommodore*, *Kommandeure*, all of the headquarters personnel, and the *Staffelkapitäne* went to Paris to celebrate. They took in the famous floor show at the "*Casino de Paris*" and ate in the "*Palais Rothschild*."

Early autumn brought typically bad weather. Wick began to look forward to going home on leave at Christmas to be with his wife and son, and his parents. But ideas were also swirling through his head. He wanted to travel around Germany, telling of the life and struggles of the fighter pilots.

A cheerful reception from comrades, and the stresses of combat are soon forgotten.

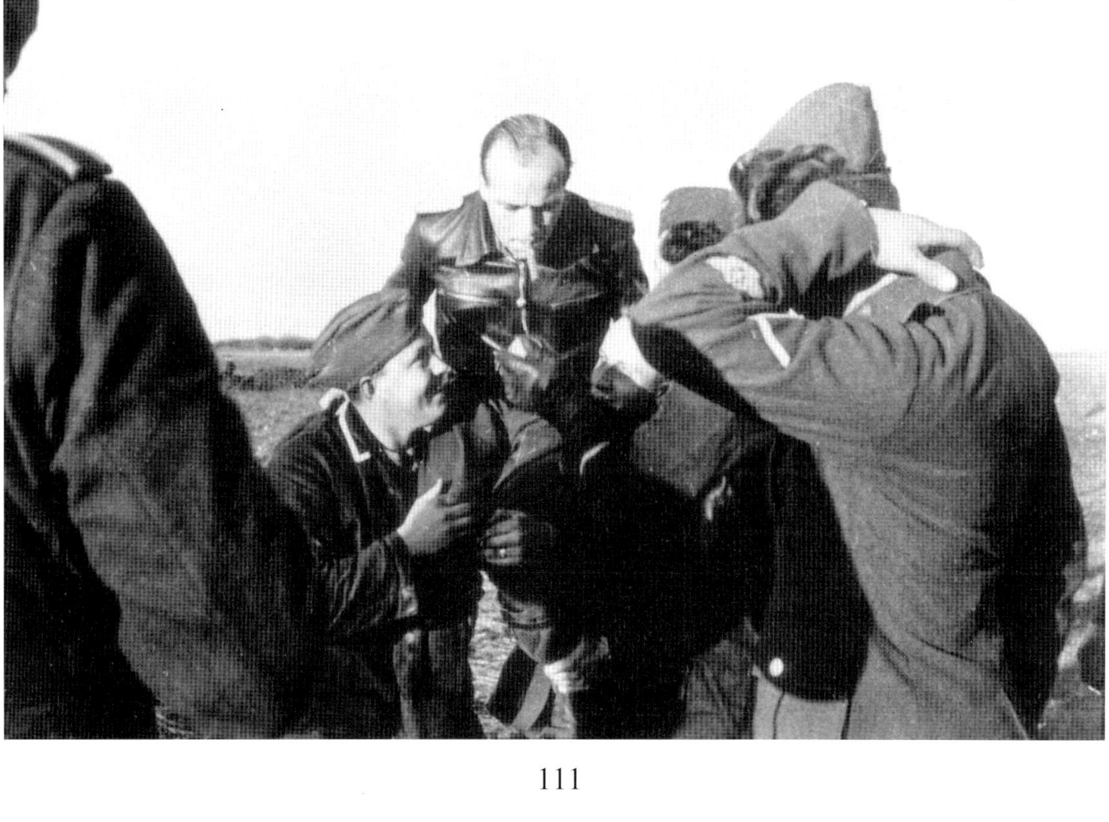

A walk on the beach in Normandy, autumn 1940.

4 November 1940. The men of JG 2, with *Major* Wick and his adjutant *Oberleutnant* Leie in the foreground, await a visit by the *Reichsmarschall*. Göring was especially fond of the *Richthofen Geschwader*, for after all he had been the unit's last commanding officer in the "Great War" following the death of von Richthofen.

The senior officers have arrived. An *Unteroffizier* carries the marshal's standard.

Reviewing the troops.

Sometimes the *Reichsmarschall* found things to criticize, even among the *Unteroffiziere*.

Göring had each of the fighter pilots state his number of combat missions and victories. From the left: Wick, Göring, unidentified, Leie, Pflanz, Krahl, Fiby, unidentified.

The *Kommodore*'s machine, still *Werknummer* 5334, here after Wick's 47th victory.

Above and Below: Helmut Wick says goodbye to a former comrade from his days in officer candidate school. In the background is the second Bf 109 E-4 used by him with an unusual form of the *Kommodore* symbol.

Wick in conversation with the imposing *Generalfeldmarschall* Hugo Sperrle, commander of *Luftflotte 3* (Air Fleet 3).

Opposite: Just before takeoff. As Wick is not wearing a life vest, this was not likely a combat mission.

Göring, Mölders, and Wick at a conference of *Geschwaderkommodore* on 9 November 1940.

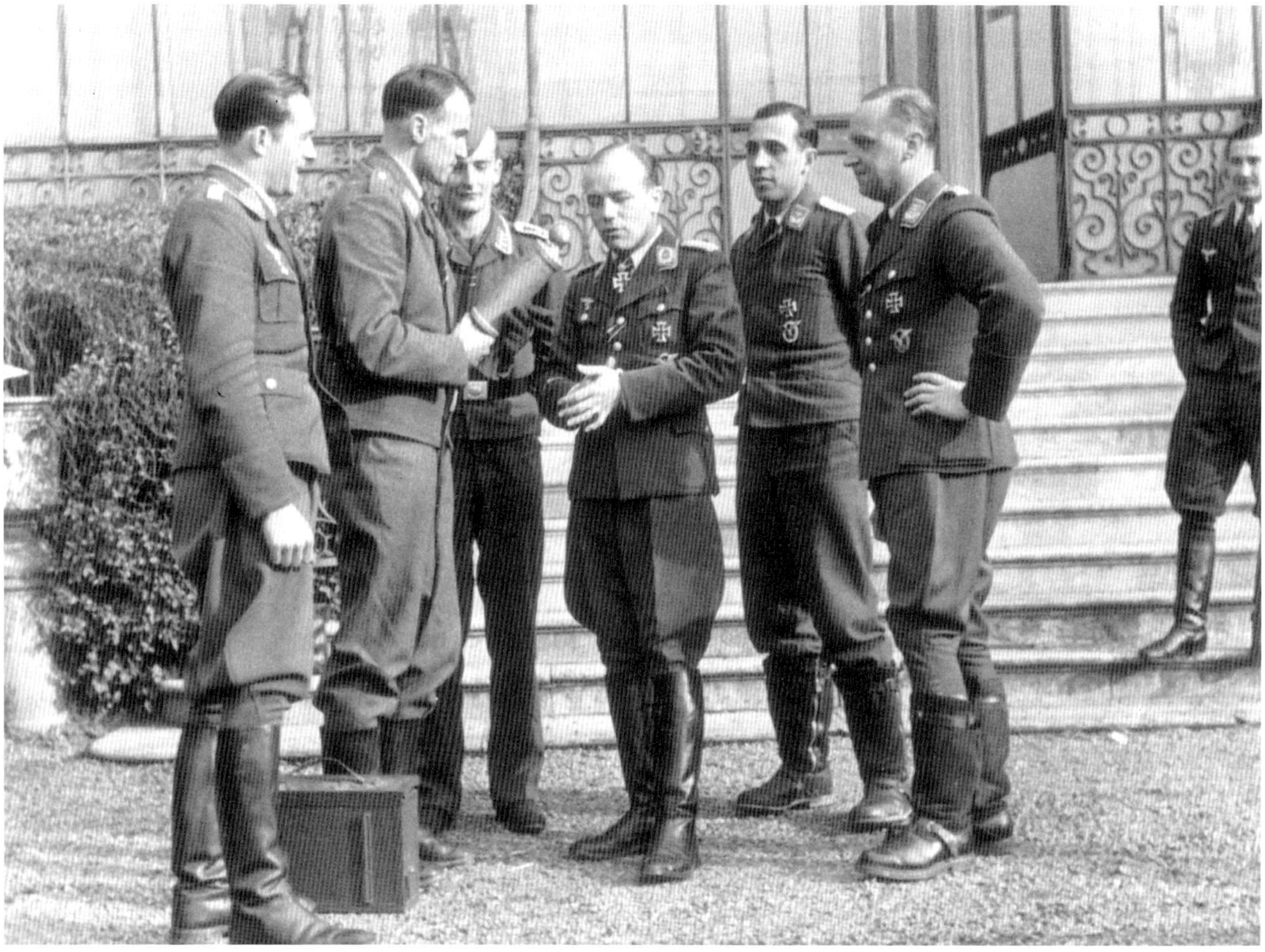

The press descended upon the *Richthofen Geschwader* again after the unit's the 500th victory, seeking information about JG 2 and its new *Kommodore*. From left: Schnell, a war correspondent, unidentified, Wick, Rudorffer, Krahl, Leie.

Major Wick speaks into the war correspondent's microphone.

Helmut Wick and Erich Leie. The two were good friends and had known each other since officer candidate school.

Wick by the tail of *Werknummer* 5344, the aircraft in which he was shot down.

The ground crews took advantage of the period of bad weather to spruce up Wick's 109 a little. The most noticeable change was the rearranged scoreboard on the aircraft's rudder. This represents the ultimate form, with 54 victory bars, as Wick scored his 55th and 56th kills on the day he was himself shot down.

Opposite: Wick after a sortie over the Channel in his second "*Kommodore* 109."

"Whoopee! I've Got a One-O-Nine!"

28 November 1940. Franz Fiby writes of Wick's last two missions on that day:

"Major Wick's last flight over England:
In the morning we flew to Cherbourg West. As I was the only one there from the *Gruppenstab*, I telephoned my old flight leader and *Kommodore* Major Wick at the fighter commander's office and asked if I might be allowed to fly in his *Schwarm*. He of course said yes. At the agreed-upon time Helmut came over our field and I joined up as number four. The flight was comprised of the following:

Schwarmführer - Kommodore Major Wick
Schwarmführer's wingman - adjutant of JG 2, *Oblt.* Leie
Element leader - technical officer of JG 2, *Oblt.* Pflanz
Element leader's wingman - adjutant I./JG 2 Lt. Fiby

Back from a mission. The little bird is once again visible, now partially covered by the chevron marking. The covered portion of the emblem was outlined in white.

We climbed to 10500 meters (the first time I had ever reached 10000). Behind us were I. and II./JG 2 and a Gruppe from JG 77. Helmut flew very fast, and Rudi (Pflanz) continuously complained over the radio that he should throttle back.

As Helmut was already almost one kilometer ahead I decided to overtake Rudi, which I did. At full boost I tried to catch up with Wick. Suddenly, I saw him open fire, and another machine, which I recognized as a Hurricane, go up in flames. I continued to close and thought about firing at a second. There were many machines above on the right with condensation trails. I assumed they were ours, but kept an eye on them. Helmut had already broken away, when suddenly one of these kites dived at me, and I recognized it as a Spitfire and saw its gleaming 'Peacock Feather Eyes' (roundels). I broke into the attack and dove away. At the same instant Rudi called a warning: 'Fibs, look out, get out of there!' He turned toward the Spitfire, which broke off its attack, so that I could have calmly carried on. Instead I roared away at 600 to 700 kph. Alone, I headed home between the sky and sea, seeing only clouds. After a long 25 minutes I made it home. The *Geschwader* had scored four victories—by Wick, Leie, Seeger, and Schuhmann—for no loss.

At 1630 hours we took off again: fighter sweep to Southampton. Once again I flew with the *Geschwaderstab*. We climbed to 10500 meters again, and over the Isle of Wight we engaged the enemy. Pflanz separated himself from the *Schwarm* during the attack, and we raced after two Spitfires. They spotted us and dove for safety, turning wildly, and we gave up the attack. We were circling, between 7000 and 8000 meters, looking for the others, when suddenly about 15 machines fell on us from above. I saw one of them turning toward Pflanz and screamed, 'Rudi, aircraft above left, we've got to get out of here!' At the same time I pushed the stick to the right and we ran for it. I lost Rudi and headed for home.

***Leutnant* Franz Fiby was a member of the *3. Staffel* for nine months. He flew 110 sorties in Wick's *Schwarm* (4 aircraft), often as his wingman. In October he was attached to the *Stab* (headquarters) of I. *Gruppe*, JG 2. As he was the only member of the *Stab* present on 28 November, he telephoned Wick at *Geschwader* headquarters and asked to be allowed to fly in the *Stabsschwarm* (headquarters flight). *Feldwebel* Stritzel was unable to fly that day, and Fiby took his place as fourth man in the flight. Thus it was that Fiby flew both missions in Helmut Wick's *Schwarm* on 28 November.**

We were still in radio contact and confirmed that we were both alright. When I was about mid-Channel I suddenly heard a *Geschwader* aircraft talking to the air-sea rescue service. A bailout had been observed southeast of Wight. I thought it was Major Wick's voice, but later I recognized it as Rudi Pflanz.

At eight in the evening I received a call, asking whether I had heard Major Wick on the radio, as he as yet hadn't landed anywhere. I drove to the *Geschwader*, where Rudi related the following: 'After I lost Fibs, I descended and headed for home. I saw two aircraft in front of me and flew toward them. Too late I recognized the second as a Spitfire. It shot down the 109 and the pilot bailed out. I shot down the Spitfire, which crashed into the sea with its pilot. Then I contacted the air-sea rescue service.'

As I wrote, in my mind I went over everything that had happened. I remembered a radio transmission that I couldn't understand. I only made out the words Major Beck, and was amazed that this name was transmitted in the clear. I suspected it was a recall order. Based on what I know now, it was Major Wick, who declared an emergency and then bailed out. I agree with Pflanz and maintain that Helmut had engine trouble (supercharger problem) and could not defend himself. I flew with Wick for eight months as his *Katschmarek* (wingman), and with Pflanz for three as element leader. We probably knew how he flew better than anyone. Helmut's way was always to disengage from the enemy at high speed, and he also maintained a good speed on the flight home, especially if there were few others with him. But as Rudi was able to overtake the Spitfire, Helmut obviously wasn't flying at high speed. Helmut had probably announced his engine problems on the radio to attract help, only I heard Beck instead of Wick. Then misfortune overtook him. In my view he had to watch as he was shot down and was unable to defend himself. I don't believe that he allowed him-

***Oberleutnant* Rudolf Pflanz, seen here wearing the Knight's Cross which he received in August 1941. He was a member of the *3. Staffel* and subsequently flew with Wick in the *Stabsschwarm* as technical officer. On 28 November 1940 he shot down the Spitfire which probably had shot down *Major* Wick. He continued to fly in the *Stabsschwarm* with Balthasar and Oesau. On 31 July 1942 he was himself shot down and killed by a Spitfire after 52 victories.**

On 28 November 1940, JG 2 adjutant *Oberleutnant* Erich Leie flew as Wick's wingman. Leie was awarded the Knight's Cross in August 1941. Tragically, he was killed near the end of the war, on 7 March 1945, as *Kommodore* of JG 77 on the Eastern Front. He had 118 victories at the time of his death.

Helmut Wick photographed in November 1940 as *Kommodore* of JG 2.

self to be taken by surprise, for he really had a 'Good Nose,' and always spotted the enemy first."

After the war, English accounts of the air fighting on 28 November shed more light on the mystery of Helmut Wick's death. They relate that No. 609 Squadron took off from Middle Wallop on its second mission that day. A large formation of German aircraft was reported precisely at tea time.

The Spitfires of 609 Squadron ran into Bf 109s at about 1710 hours. Pilot Officer Keith Ogilvy was flying in the high position behind the squadron. Glancing at his rearview mirror, he saw three yellow-nosed Bf 109s in close formation on his tail. He immediately warned his comrades. The leading Messerschmitt opened fire, and Ogilvy dove away, with several strikes in his aircraft's fuselage. Pilot Officer Paul Baillon had no luck, however, and was shot down. Ogilvy saw Baillon bail out. His parachute opened, and he landed in the sea about 20 miles south of Bournemouth. Ogilvy saw no signs of life, however. Flight Lieutenant Dundas excitedly announced the downing of a Messerschmitt. His comrades heard him broadcast, "Whoopee! I've got a one-o-nine!" Squadron Leader Robinson answered, "Good show, John.". But John Dundas didn't answer. His victory report was his last his comrades would ever hear from him. A few minutes after the start of the battle the Spitfires of No. 152 Squadron joined the proceedings. One of that squadron's pilots was Pilot Officer Eric Marrs. He ob-

Pilot Officer Paul Baillon, Wick's 56th and last victim. His body washed ashore on the Normandy coast on 5 January 1941 and he was buried near Bayeux with military honors. Like Ursel Wick, Baillon's wife was expecting a child.

served a Bf 109 that dove away and flew in the direction of France. Marrs closed to within about 100 yards (90 meters) and fired a short burst at the German. Oil from the Messerschmitt immediately covered his windscreen, and he lost sight of the 109. While trying to regain sight of his opponent, he suddenly saw a parachute and pieces of wreckage, which he assumed were from the Messerschmitt. 152 Squadron lost two Spitfires in this action, flown by Sergeant Klein, a Pole, and Pilot Officer Watson. Both were killed. Marrs may have seen a shot-down Spitfire, and the Messerschmitt he had attacked just made it home. According to *Oberleutnant* Pflanz, the only Spitfire that actually scored a kill was shot down by himself. Marrs may have been confused, which easily happens in air combat. Nos. 609 and 152 Squadrons lost four Spitfires and four pilots in this action. Pilot Officer Baillon was *Major* Wick's 56th and last victim.

A portrait of Flight Lieutenant John Charles Dundas, known to his friends as "Dos" or "Scruffy". In civilian life a successful journalist with the Yorkshire Post and since May 1938 a member of No. 609 Squadron. He is believed to have shot down *Major* Wick on 28 November 1940—his 13th victory. It was to be his last, however, for Dundas was himself shot down almost immediately, probably by *Oberleutnant* Pflanz. Dundas wore the DFC with Bar. He, too, is officially listed as missing.

Nummer 48 28. November 1940

Berliner Illustrirte Zeitung

49. Jahrgang Preis 20 Pfennig

Der Reichsmarschall besucht das Jagdgeschwader Richthofen

Wick appeared on the cover of the big Berlin daily newspaper *Berlin Illustrated News* for the second time on 28 November 1940, the very day he was killed in action.

Missing
An Announcement by the *Wehrmacht* High Command

One after another, the Bf 109 Es of *JG "Richthofen" Nr. 2* landed at various French airfields. It took some time to determine who was missing. It was already getting dark, and two aircraft were overdue—*Oberleutnant* Pflanz and *Major* Wick. Pflanz reported in by telephone: he had landed in a field, almost out of fuel. His report on the downed Messerschmitt left no doubt as to who was missing—the *Kommodore* himself. *Oberleutnant* Leie informed the *Reichsmarschall*. Furious, Göring demanded the combat report immediately. That same night he set in motion everything possible to rescue his young *Kommodore* from the water. By order of the *Kriegsmarine*'s commanding admiral, torpedo boats put to sea from Cherbourg. The rescue boats normally used were not equipped for night operation, and as well a storm was brewing over the sea—by that time the sea state had reached Level 8. Every station, every post, from Le Havre to Brest that might have anything to do with the incident was contacted.

The men of the *Richthofen Geschwader* looked hopefully toward the coming day. They believed that Wick might yet be found; after all, he had an inflatable raft and dye packet with him. Perhaps the English had already fished him out. While that would have been bad luck, it was still better than death.

29 November: The night search was fruitless. Aircraft of the *Geschwader* and air-sea rescue aircraft took to the air to search for Helmut Wick. Light naval forces put to sea as well. Reconnaissance aircraft flew low over the coast of the Isle of Wight. Some of the fighters escorted the air-sea rescue aircraft, while the rest flew low looking for their *Kommodore*. Rudi Pflanz led the *Stabsschwarm* to the spot where the drama had been played out the day before. Fifty kilometers from that spot two oily patches were sighted close together on the water, probably left by the two downed fighter aircraft. Taking into account the currents in that area (Pflanz had checked with the navy), the search was continued from the area of the oil patches. Other than the oil, however, no clue was found to Wick's whereabouts. The search continued in the afternoon, and *Leutnant* Meimberg shot down a Bristol Blenheim. All four crewmembers were killed.

Of *Major* Wick, however, there was still no sign. As a result, more attention was paid to the possibility that Wick may have been rescued by the English. Hermann Göring had an inquiry made of the RAF as to whether Wick was a prisoner of war. Two days later the English replied that no *Major* Wick had been captured in the past few days. A short time later British radio broadcast news of Wick's loss, adding, "...thus Hitler has again sent one of his best to his death!"

On 29 November Franz Fiby wrote in his diary:

"The *Geschwader* is searching for its *Kommodore*. Search flights were carried out throughout the day. Air-sea rescue aircraft flew 22 sorties and we flew escort, while some carried out a low-level search. We were determined to retrieve our *Kommodore*—who had a life raft with him—alive or dead. But apart from two large patches of oil, which must have come from the two aircraft, we found nothing. The *Reichsmarschall* ordered all of the navy's ships on the Channel to put to sea the first night. Everything was tried. Unfortunately it was all unsuccessful, a unique display of hero worship about which the rest of the world remained unaware."

It is known for certain that Wick shot his 56th victim out of the sky and then dove away. What happened then is still not clearly understood, and will probably always remain so. After the war Franz Fiby could not remember any definitive statement ever having been made concerning the events surrounding Helmut Wick. Rudi Pflanz had seen the attack on Wick, however, he could not say what happened afterward. Only later did it become a tragic probability that it had been Wick in the "109" he saw crash. Reports about *Major* Wick, such as the four-part series on his life published in the *Luftwaffe* magazine *Der Adler* in late 1940-early 1941, were based on *Oberleutnant* Pflanz's statements. The book *Helmut Wick - Das Leben eines Fliegerhelden*, which appeared in 1943, contains a similar account of Wick's last mission.

Erich Rudorffer tells a different story. To this day, Rudorffer claims that he had a clear view of Wick's final moments. His version: he was the fourth man in the *Geschwaderstab*, replacing *Feldwebel* Seeger. Wick was shot down on the first mission and was still in the cockpit when the aircraft hit the water. After returning and reporting the incident, Rudorffer received a severe dressing down from Göring over the phone, after which he took off again to search for Wick. Take-off time of the second sortie on 28 November: 1630 hours, landing at 1720. His log entry contains the remark: contact with Spitfires in the area of the Isle of Wight. In his version, all other statements about Wick's loss were part of a cover-up. However, Rudorffer's version is disputed by other eyewitnesses. It is said that he refused to talk about the past for a long time following the war, and it may be assumed that his memory of events became confused. On that 28 November *Feldwebel* (later *Unteroffizier*) Seeger was a member of the *3. Staffel*, but only flew the first mission, and not until later did he join the *Stabsschwarm* under *Major* Oesau. Franz Fiby's writings in his log book and diary clearly tell another story. On that day *Leutnant* Fiby replaced *Stabsfeldwebel* Stritzel, while Rudorffer flew with the *2. Staffel*. Rudorffer's recorded flight time of 50 minutes for the second mission is too short for him to have even taken part in the combat in question. For according to German and English reports, the two fighter formations met over the western tip of the Isle of Wight at about 1710 hours, while

A German pilot in his life raft.

A high speed launch operated by the British air-sea rescue service.

One of the rescue floats the Germans anchored in the English Channel.

A Heinkel He 59 of the German Red Cross air-sea rescue service. Although they were clearly marked as rescue aircraft, many were shot down in the combat zone by order of British Prime Minister Churchill. In mid-1940 the aircraft were camouflaged and fitted with light defensive armament.

Rudorffer's log book states that he landed at Cherbourg-West at 1720.* This would have allowed him just 10 minutes to search, engage the enemy, fly approximately 100 kilometers back to base, and land!

Erich Leie and Rudolf Pflanz drove to Berlin to break the news to Helmut's wife and parents. It was no easy task, for they were having a difficult time as it was dealing with his loss.

An announcement by the *Wehrmacht* High Command: 4 December 1940: the Kommodore of Jagdgeschwader Richthofen, Major Wick, failed to return from a combat operation after recording his 56th victory. Thus the German air force has lost one of its most skilled and successful fighter pilots. Major Wick, who was decorated with the Knight's Cross with Oak Leaves for his heroic actions in the struggle for the future of the German people, will live on as an example to the German people and especially to German youth.

Helmut Wick's closest comrades missed him, to say nothing of his family, especially his wife. But there was also sadness on the other side of the Channel. Like Wick, Flight Lieutenant John Charles Dundas was never found.

Both sides had lost one of their most successful fighter pilots. Dundas was one of RAF Fighter Command's top pilots and led No. 609 Squadron in victories. He had been a member of 609 Squadron since May 1938. He scored his first kill over Dunkirk on 31 May 1940, shooting down a He 111. His total (the RAF used a different, but no less accurate, method of counting victories) from 31 May to 28 November 1940 was 13 confirmed kills and two probables. Dundas had shared in four other victories, damaged four enemy aircraft, and shared in the damaging of another. In civilian life John Dundas had been a talented, up and coming reporter for the Yorkshire Post. Like Wick, he was convinced that he was fighting for a just cause. Dundas was an intellectual with a tendency to be the

*With a total of 222 victories, *Major* Erich Rudorffer is seventh on the list of German fighter aces. He also holds the record for the most enemy aircraft shot down in a single mission, 13 (as *Hauptmann* on 6 Nov. 1943). He flew with *Jagdgeschwader 2, 54* (Green Heart), and *7*, the latter equipped with the Me 262 (12 victories). For more information on this pilot see Toliver/Constable: *Das waren die deutschen Jagdflieger-Asse*, Motorbuch Verlag, Stuttgart, 1995 (15th edition).

Erich Rudorffer (left). He claimed that Wick was in fact shot down during the first mission on 28 November.

The small castle in Beaumont-le-Roger in early December 1940. Out of respect, the blinds of *Major* Wick's office were left rolled down for several days.

Wick's office, decorated like a grave.

Wick's place at the dining table was left empty for some time.

best at whatever he did, including piloting a fighter. Like Wick he was willing to take risks, had a stubborn streak, and was prone to recklessness. On 27 November 1940, for example, he pursued a Ju 88 across the Channel to Cherbourg, contrary to strict orders, and shot it down in flames. Not until he spotted a nearby airfield crowded with Bf 109s did he beat a hasty retreat.

John Dundas' brother Hugh, also an RAF fighter pilot, later wrote in his book:

"It was the last encounter of the year, at squadron strength, between Spitfires and Messerschmitts. It certainly contributed nothing, one way or the other, to the course or outcome of the war. But it affected my life deeply. I think that hardly a day has gone by since then when I have not thought of John."

Pilot Officer Baillon was *Major* Wick's 56th and last victim. He had come straight from a training school and joined 609 Squadron on 28 September. One month later, on 27 October, he was shot down for the first time, by return fire from a Ju 88. Baillon bailed out and survived the incident unharmed. In civilian life he was a lawyer, a quiet, modest man. On 28 November he was shot down by Helmut Wick and again took to his parachute. A month later, on 1 January 1941, Paul Baillon's body washed up on the French coast. The Germans buried him with military honors. Baillon's wife was expecting a child, as was Wick's.

Major Wick vermißt

Von einem Feindflug gegen England nicht zurückgekehrt

Major Wick, der Kommodore des bekannten Richthofen-Geschwaders und Träger des Ritterkreuzes mit Eichenlaub, ist am 28. November von einem Feindflug, auf dem er seinen 56. Gegner abschoß, nicht zurückgekehrt und wird seitdem vermißt.

*

Die militärische Laufbahn des Kommodore des ruhmreichen Geschwaders, das den Namen Richthofen trägt und Erinnerung an unsterblichen Heldentaten aus dem Weltkrieg wie eine Fahne mit sich führt, war von dem fliegerischen Einsatz einer der Besten und Mutigsten der deutschen Luftwaffe bestimmt. Am 1. September 1938 wurde Wick zum Leutnant ernannt. Noch innerhalb von zwei Jahren rückte der Fliegerleutnant auf der militärischen Laufbahn bis zum Major und zum Kommodore des siegreichen Geschwaders auf. Am 1. September 1940 — Wick hatte seinen 20. Luftsieg erfochten — bekam er vom Reichsmarschall Göring persönlich das Ritterkreuz zum Eisernen Kreuz überreicht. Er ist dann der vierte Offizier der gesamten deutschen Wehrmacht, der das Eichenlaub zum Ritterkreuz vom Führer erhalten hat. Inmitten seiner Kameraden bekommt er das Telegramm des Führers: „In dankbarer Würdigung ihres heldenhaften Einsatzes, im Kampf für die Zukunft unseres Volkes", in dem ihm die Verleihung des Eichenlaubes mitgeteilt wird. Der Führer empfing Major Wick, um ihm selbst die große Ehrenauszeichnung zu übergeben.

Immer wieder zog Wick aus zum Feindflug. Immer wieder begleitete ihn der Sieg. 56 Gegner holt der große deutsche Flieger aus der Luft, eine nüchterne Zahl, aber welche Unsumme von Tapferkeit, stets bereitem Einsatzwillen und hohem soldatischen Können birgt diese stolze Siegesziffer!

Die Kameraden des strahlenden, siegreichen Soldaten und das deutsche Volk aber können die letzte Hoffnung nicht aufgeben, daß doch noch einmal eine gute Nachricht von dem vermißten Fliegerhelden eintrifft.

Major Wick

Scherl-Bilderdienst

One of the countless press reports about the loss of the then most successful German fighter pilot, *Major* Helmut Wick.

Brothers Hugh and John Dundas, both fighter pilots in the RAF.

On 16 February 1941 *Hauptmann* Wilhelm Balthasar assumed command of JG 2. On 3 July he, too, was killed.

***

With 56 victories, at the time of his death Helmut Wick was one of the most successful fighter pilots, and probably the brightest star in the *Luftwaffe*. It may seem tragic that Wick had to die under such unfortunate circumstances at the height of his career. If two unconfirmed eyewitness statements are to be believed, then the circumstances were in fact much more tragic. For on that fateful day, Hermann Göring is said to have sent an order to JG 2 at Beaumont-le-Roger, temporarily forbidding *Major* Wick from taking part in further combat operations. The order arrived too late. This is plausible, for Wick could have provided a valuable service training new pilots. There is also a statement that Wick took off on his final sortie without a dye packet or cartridges for his flare pistol. A member of the ground crew is said to have pointed out to Wick that the equipment was missing, whereupon he just winked and said, "Oh, let's leave it!" Was this the arrogance of a seemingly invincible Siegfried? True or not, the story would fit Helmut Wick.

Wick's loss was a heavy blow to the men of JG 2. *Hauptmann* Greisert temporarily assumed command of the *Richthofen Geschwader* until *Hauptmann* Balthasar took over on 16 February.

Opposite: Helmut Wick remains missing to the present day.

Epilogue

On 4 December Helmut Wick was officially declared dead in a *Wehrmacht* communiquÈ. But even dead heroes had propaganda value, and not just in Germany. Fighter pilots and submarine commanders, in particular, were elevated to the status of stars. Newspaper articles, radio reports, books and postcards inspired many young Germans to follow in the footsteps of their heroes. The war went on, and other stars appeared in the fighting firmament—shining brightly and then fading.

Hetzjagd am HIMMEL

von Major Helmuth Wick

I. Der erste Luftsieg

Above and opposite: After Wick was reported missing, many newspapers and illustrated news magazines published accounts of the young *Major*'s life, including *Der Adler* (The Eagle) and the *Illustrierte Beobachter* (Illustrated Observer).

Preis: 20 Pfennig
Frankreich 4 frs.
Ausland mit ermäß. Porto 30 Pfg. Italien 2 Lire, Schweiz 40 Rappen, Spanien Pias. 1.25, Portugal 2,– Esc., Ungarn Pengö –.52, Belgien 2 blrs., Holland 15 Cts. Jugoslavien 4 Dinar, Bulgarien 10 Lewa.

DONNERSTAG, 23. JANUAR 1941
16. JAHRGANG •• FOLGE 4

IB Illustrierter Beobachter

AUS DEM INHALT
NSKK. macht Flandernbeute nutzbar / Kinder besuchen unsere Flak / Japan 2600 Jahre Kaiserreich / Schlangenfraß
u. a. m.

VERLAG FRANZ EHER NACHF. GMBH MÜNCHEN 22

Sieger an Englands Himmel.
Kommodore Helmut Wick als Oberleutnant im Westen. Hier schildert er einem Kriegsberichter Erlebnisse von seinem jüngsten Feindflug.
Zu unserem Tatsachenbericht, der in diesem Heft beginnt

Aufnahme: PK. Sturm (Scherl-Bilderdienst)

Obviously Helmut Wick still had admirers among student pilots in 1943, as the legend on this Kranich (Crane) glider clearly shows. The misspelling of Wick's last name probably wasn't noticed.

In January 1941 Helmut Wick's father received a call from *Führer* Headquarters with unexpected good news. The following is an extract from a letter written by Ursel Wick to his son on 26 January 1941:

"On 23 January the Führer's adjutant, *Generalleutnant* Bodenschatz, telephoned Wick Sr. and informed him on behalf of the Führer of an official Reuters report that a 25-year-old Luftwaffe Major, credited with 56 victories and one of the three best airmen in Göring's air force, had been delivered to an internment camp in Canada. Bodenschatz also said that the Führer was very happy and excited, declaring several times that the joy he experienced on receiving this news was the greatest he had felt for a long time. Mother and Ursel immediately went to Wannsee to discuss this good news with father Wick. Soon afterwards someone called from an office—I can't remember which one—and said that the *Reichsmarschall* wanted to speak to Frau Wick. I had the call transferred to the Wicks, and after Ursel's return late that night she told me that Hermann Göring had said the same thing to her that the Führer had told me through Bodenschatz. The news is still not official, but both the Führer and Göring immediately initiated steps to receive official confirmation. And the accompanying translation of articles from American newspapers leaves no doubt that it could only be our Helmut. Those are the facts. Now we have to wait a while longer and hope that these final doubts will also be taken from us."

An American newspaper article reported at the beginning of 1941:

"The miraculous rescue of Major Wick.

The American agency Associated Press reported from a port in Eastern Canada that a 25-year-old combat pilot credited with 56 victories since the start of the Spanish Civil War was delivered there as a prisoner of war. His name was kept secret in keeping with Canadian methods of handling prisoners of war. The prisoner of war wears the Knight's Cross with Oak Leaves. He was shot down by English pilots over the Channel. In a commentary the New York Times newspaper pointed out that the description fits Major Wick."

Above: Ursel Wick with little Walter. Her second child, a girl, was already on the way. Below: Ursel Wick and a friend. Until the end of 1941 Ursel waited in vain for news from Canada, where her husband was allegedly being held as a prisoner of war.

Franz Fiby, long after the war. He was good friends with Helmut Wick. Without his help this book would not have been possible. His personal writings in the form of two diaries, and his photo album were the basis of this work. The book *Helmut Wick—Das Leben eines Fliegerhelden* (*Helmut Wick – Life of a Flying Hero*), published in 1943, was also based in large part on Franz Fiby's diaries. Contrary to claims at the time, Wick himself kept no diary. About Helmut Wick's behavior, especially after contacting the enemy, Fiby remarked: "Wick was a real daredevil. He had excellent eyesight and therefore was usually the first to see enemy aircraft. Then he opened the throttle and simply went after them. I didn't do that, but that's probably why I'm still alive and he isn't."

But all hopes of seeing Helmut again went unfulfilled. On 5 February 1941 a telegram was received from Ottawa: "According to official information Major Wick is not interned in Canada – stop – Press report incorrect – stop."

In spite of this Ursel Wick kept writing to Canada and the USA until the end of 1941—in vain. Her husband did not return, and the press report in fact turned out to be false. In 1941 she brought her second child into the world. She remarried during the war. Her second husband, a military doctor, did not like to hear talk of Helmut—the subject was taboo in the family. Ursel Wick died unexpectedly in 1968 at the age of just 52.

Appendix A:
List of Helmut Wick's Victories

Nr.	Date	Type	Location
1	22.11.39	Curtiss 75A	Nancy
shared	30.4.40	Potez 63	Trier
2	17.5.40	LeO 45	Rethel
3	17.5.40	LeO 45	Rethel
4	17.5.40	LeO 45	Rethel
unconfirmed	19.5.40	Swordfish	Calais
unconfirmed	19.5.40	Swordfish	Calais
5	5.6.40	Bloch 151/152	Compiègne
6	5.6.40	Bloch 151/152	Compiègne
7	5.6.40	Bloch 151/152	Compiègne
8	5.6.40	Bloch 151/152	Compiègne
9	6.6.40	Bloch 151/152	Reims
10	6.6.40	Bloch 151/152	Reims
11	8.6.40	Bloch 151/152	Soissons
12	8.6.40	Morane M.S. 406	Soissons
13	9.6.40	Blenheim	Soissons
14	13.6.40	Battle	Montdidier
15	17.7.40	Spitfire	east of Brighton
16	11.8.40	Curtiss P 36	Portland
17	11.8.40	Spitfire	Portland
18	11.8.40	Hurricane	Portland
19	16.8.40	Hurricane	
20	24.8.40	Hurricane	
21	25.8.40	Spitfire	Portland
22	25.8.40	Hurricane	
23	4.9.40	Hurricane	Kent
24	4.9.40	Hurricane	Kent
25	5.9.40	Spitfire	Canterbury
26	6.9.40	Spitfire	Dover
27	7.9.40		
28	8.9.40		
29	8.9.40		
30	8.9.40		
31	9.9.40		Kanal
32	9.9.40		Kanal
33	30.9.40	Spitfire	Portland
34	30.9.40	Spitfire	Portland
35	3.10.40	Spitfire	Swanage
36	3.10.40	Spitfire	Swanage
37	5.10.40	Hurricane	Southamton
38	5.10.40	Hurricane	Southamton
39	5.10.40	Hurricane	Southamton
40	5.10.40	Spitfire	south of Portland
41	5.10.40	Spitfire	south of Portland
42	?.10.40		
43	29.10.40		
44	29.10.40		
45	5.11.40	Hurricane	
46	5.11.40	Hurricane	
47	5.11.40	Spitfire	
48	6.11.40	Hurricane	Southamton
49	6.11.40	Hurricane	Southamton
50	6.11.40	Spitfire	east of Isle of Wight
51	6.11.40	Spitfire	east of Isle of Wight
52	6.11.40	Spitfire	east of Isle of Wight
53	7.11.40		
54	9.11.40		
55	28.11.40		Isle of Wight
56	28.11.40		Isle of Wight

Appendix B:

Brief Description of the Aircraft Types Shot Down by Wick

Curtiss Hawk 75 A (designated P-36 by the Americans and Mohawk by the British) – single-engined, single-seat fighter. The RAF claims that it did not employ the Curtiss fighters on operations in the summer and fall of 1940. German pilots nevertheless claimed to have shot down examples of this radial-engined fighter,, which they had earlier encountered over France.
Potez 63 – twin-engined reconnaissance aircraft, bomber and fighter, crew of two or three.
Lioré et Olivier LeO 45 – twin-engined bomber of modern design, crew of four.
Fairey Swordfish – single-engined biplane torpedo bomber, crew of two or three.
Bloch 151/152 – single-engined, single-seat fighter.
Morane-Saulnier M.S. 406 – single-engined, single-seat fighter.
Bristol Blenheim – twin-engined light bomber, reconnaissance aircraft and night-fighter, crew of three.
Fairey Battle – single-engined light bomber, crew of three.
Hawker Hurricane – single-engined, single-seat fighter.
Supermarine Spitfire – single-engined, single-seat fighter.

Like those of many other *Luftwaffe* fighter pilots, doubts have been expressed about some of Helmut Wick's victories. Postwar comparisons between victory claims and actual losses have generally revealed significant differences between claims and losses. Wick's were no different. The procedure for confirming victories differed from one *Jagdgeschwader* to another. In the heat of battle it was entirely possible for two pilots to claim the same aircraft shot down—no matter which side they were on. In theory, however, *Luftwaffe* fighter pilots required a witness for a victory to be confirmed. Occasionally an aircraft was seen to go down and was claimed as a victory, when in fact it was only damaged. Whether his true total was 56 or perhaps only 50, in 1940 Helmut Wick was an absolute exception among fighter pilots, and in fact had no need to claim "uncertain" victories.

Wick was, however, definitely determined to surpass his two closest rivals in the *Luftwaffe*, Mölders and Galland, and become number one in the German fighter universe.

Appendix C:
Aircraft Flown by Helmut Wick and His Adversaries

While serving in the *Luftwaffe* Helmut Wick flew a wide variety of aircraft types. With *Jagdgeschwader 53* and *Jagdgeschwader 2* he flew the Bf 109 almost exclusively (Bf stood for Bayerische Flugzeugwerke AG, for whom the famous designer Willi Messerschmitt designed the Bf 109. In mid-1938 the abbreviation changed to Me and this was associated with all subsequent Messerschmitt designs. Colloquially the Bf 109 was sometimes designated Me 109 or just 109; however, Messerschmitt Bf 109 remained the correct designation.)

The vast majority of photographs showing Helmut Wick with an aircraft depict his second Bf 109, *Werknummer* 5344, which he flew while serving with JG 2. It was this aircraft in which he was shot down. There were occasions, however, when pilots flew aircraft other than their own, depending on which aircraft were serviceable and which pilots were assigned to fly a particular mission.

Two contemporary enemy fighters, the Hawker Hurricane Mk. I and Supermarine Spitfire Mk. I are also depicted in the following pages.

As many inaccurate depictions of Helmut Wick's Messerschmitt Bf 109 exist, I hope that the following side-views will provide some clarification. In many cases, contradictory statements by contemporary witnesses and the always difficult task of evaluating black and white photographs make it impossible to be dogmatic about an aircraft's appearance. I should be very grateful if any reader can provide additional information.

87
2

HORRIDO
2

Leutnant Wick's Bf 109 E-3 in the winter of 1939-40 at Frankfurt-Rebstock. It was painted in the then typical scheme of RLM 65 (pale blue) undersides and fuselage sides, with the upper surfaces in a splinter scheme of RLM 71 (dark green) and RLM 02 (RLM gray). Spinner and propeller blades were RLM 70 (black green). The fuselage sides were later overpainted in dark green. The aircraft still wore the narrow Balkenkreuz with swastika national emblem in the center of the fin and rudder. Wick's personal emblem, a little bird, was painted on the left side of the fuselage. The Horrido emblem did not appear on the engine cowling until spring 1940. The aircraft was written off after it accidentally rolled down a hill. There were twelve victory bars on its tail at that time.

Oberleutnant Wick's Bf 109 E-4, "Yellow 2", *Werknummer* 5344, as it appeared in early September 1940, when Wick was *Kapitän* of the *3. Staffel* of JG 2 based at Mardyck, Belgium. The aircraft's camouflage scheme again consisted of RLM 65 with a splinter scheme of RLM 71 and RLM 02. Most of the pale blue on the fuselage sides was later overpainted with dark green. The Balkenkreuz was also changed, with the outer black lines made considerably thicker. The underwing crosses were similarly modified. The propeller and spinner were RLM 71 dark green instead of RLM 70 black green. The *3. Staffel* emblem, the blue Horrido pennant, appeared on both sides of the fuselage as did the *Geschwader* emblem. This "Yellow 2" also bore the little bird emblem, although its shape and color were somewhat different than before.

HORRIDO

HORRIDO

***Hauptmann* Wick's Messerschmitt Bf 109 E-4, *Werknummer* 5344, as used by him while *Kommandeur* of *I. Gruppe* of JG 2 in September and October 1940 at Beaumont-le-Roger. The "Yellow 2" had given way to the double chevrons of a *Gruppenkommandeur*. The engine cowling and spinner were probably overall white at first. Later they, and part of the rudder, were painted RLM Yellow 04. Compared to photographs of other aircraft with yellow cowlings, the yellow on Wick's machine seems quite pale. Perhaps the yellow color did not cover properly. When the cowling was repainted yellow, the rear portion of the spinner was left white.**

Technical Information Bf 109 E-3/4 (E-1)
Length: 8.76 m. Wingspan: 9.90 m. Wing area: 16.40 m2. Gross weight: approx. 2 600 kg. Maximum speed: approx. 560 kph at 4 400 m. Rate of climb: 950 m/min. Service ceiling: approx. 11 000 m. Range: approx. 660 km.
Power Plant: one liquid-cooled Daimler-Benz DB 601 A inverted-vee twelve-cylinder motor producing 1,175 h.p. (1,100 h.p.) for takeoff.
Armament: two 7.9-mm MG 17 machine-guns above the engine and two 20-mm MG FF cannon (two MG 17) in the wings. A very small number of aircraft were also equipped with an engine-mounted MG FF cannon.

The Bf 109 "Emil" was an outstanding fighter aircraft by the standards of 1940. Its fuel-injected DB 601 allowed the Messerschmitt to push over into a dive, unlike its greatest rival the Spitfire. It also possessed a superior rate of climb to an altitude of about 5 500 meters. Both the Spitfire and Hurricane could outturn the Messerschmitt, thanks to their lower wing loading, and German pilots were well advised to avoid dogfighting. One weakness of the Bf 109 was its narrow and relatively unstable undercarriage. The aircraft also had rather difficult takeoff and landing characteristics, demanding the pilot's full attention. These two factors resulted in numerous accidents.

HORRIDO

HORRIDO

Major Wick's Bf 109 E-4, *Werknummer* 5344, as it appeared at the beginning of November 1940 when he was *Kommodore* of JG 2 based at Beaumont-le-Roger. The *Gruppenkommandeur*'s chevrons have been roughly overpainted and the insignia of a *Kommodore* applied. Note that the armor glass panel has been removed from in front of the windscreen.
The second view shows how the aircraft looked after 9 November. The victory bars, 54 altogether, have been repainted. As well, the entire rudder has been painted yellow and lightly dappled with RLM 71 dark green. As depicted, the engine cowling has received a similar treatment, but this is just an assumption. The spinner and propeller were black green. Wick was shot down in this aircraft on 28 November.

Wick's personal emblem as it appeared on *Werknummer* 5344. It could be a kingfisher, a bird known for its aerobatics and hunting skills. The little bird was also considered a good luck charm. The colors shown here are based on those of a kingfisher—as to colors of the Wick original, however, one can only speculate.

This aircraft is another Messerschmitt Bf 109 E-4 flown by Wick as *Kommodore*, *Werknummer* unknown. Based on available photos, it differed from the *Kommodore*'s other aircraft in having normal fuselage crosses, a rather unusual form of the *Kommodore* insignia, and an outline form of the *Geschwader* emblem with no white background.

It may have been painted in the scheme of RLM 71 and RLM 02 above, with RLM 65 sides and under surfaces, which was applied by the manufacturer at that time. The sides also received a mottled finish in RLM 02 and 71. It is not known if victory bars and the little bird emblem were painted on this machine. It is unlikely, however, as the Horrido emblem is absent from the engine cowling.

The Horrido Pennant was initially the personal emblem of *Hauptmann* Henning Strümpell, *Kapitän* of the *3. Staffel* of JG 2, and beginning in the spring of 1940 it became the emblem of all of 3./JG 2. It was not, as is often stated, Wick's personal emblem! When Strümpell left the *3. Staffel* to take over the *I. Gruppe*, Wick—now *Kapitän* of 3./JG 2 himself—asked if the *Staffel* might retain the emblem. Strümpell replied that he didn't mind. Wick retained the emblem on his aircraft even after he became *Kommandeur* and then *Kommodore*.

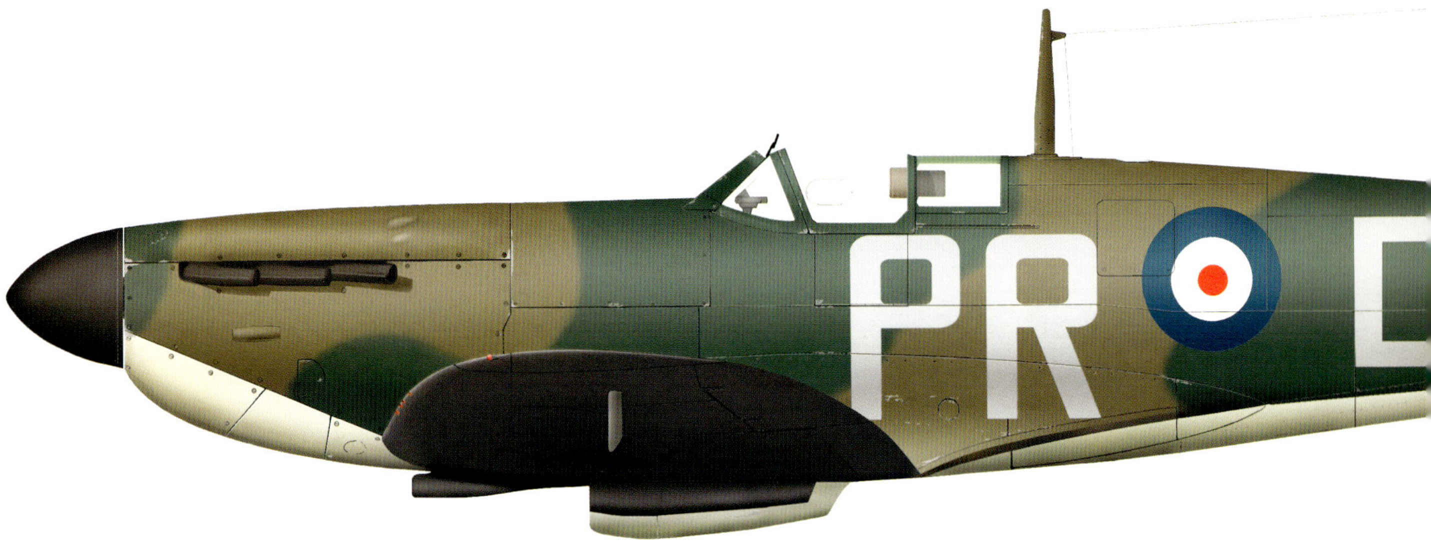

Technical Information Spitfire Mk. IA:
(production of the Mk. II began in June 1940)
Length: 9.12 m. Wingspan: 11.23 m. Wing area: 22.48 m2. Gross weight: approx. 2 650 kg. Maximum speed: approx. 560 (570) kph at 5 600 m.2 Rate of climb: 750 (850) m/min. Service ceiling: approx. 10 500 m (11 000 m). Range: approx. 670 km. Power Plant: one liquid-cooled Rolls-Royce Merlin V-12 engine producing 1,030 (1,175) h.p. Armament: eight .303 inch Browning machine-guns in the wings.

Supermarine Spitfire Mk. IA, PR-D, R6769 at the beginning of August 1940. It belonged to No. 609 Squadron, which was based at Middle Wallop and Warmwell from July to December. The fighters of No. 609 Squadron were thus direct opponents of JG 2 in the airspace around the Isle of Wight. The aircraft was damaged in a bombing raid on 12 August, but was quickly repaired and subsequently flew with No. 609 Squadron until 10 September, when it was taken on strength by No. 64 Squadron. John Dundas also flew this aircraft, claiming a Bf 110 as a probable with it on 25 August.

The fuselage roundel does not have the yellow outer ring introduced in the spring of 1940 and the underside of the port wing is still black. See also the two Spitfires on Page 42, also flown by No. 609 Squadron.

To this day in England the Spitfire remains a symbol of the Battle of Britain, and in the summer of 1940 it and the Messerschmitt Bf 109 were probably the best fighter aircraft anywhere. Its advantages were its high speed combined with excellent maneuverability at all altitudes. The Spitfire was superior to the Bf 109 E at heights above 6 000 meters and was also able to outturn the Messerschmitt. One serious disadvantage of the early Merlin engines was their carburetion system. When placed under negative g, the engine would simply cut out. To avoid this, the pilot had to roll the aircraft onto its back before diving at full power.

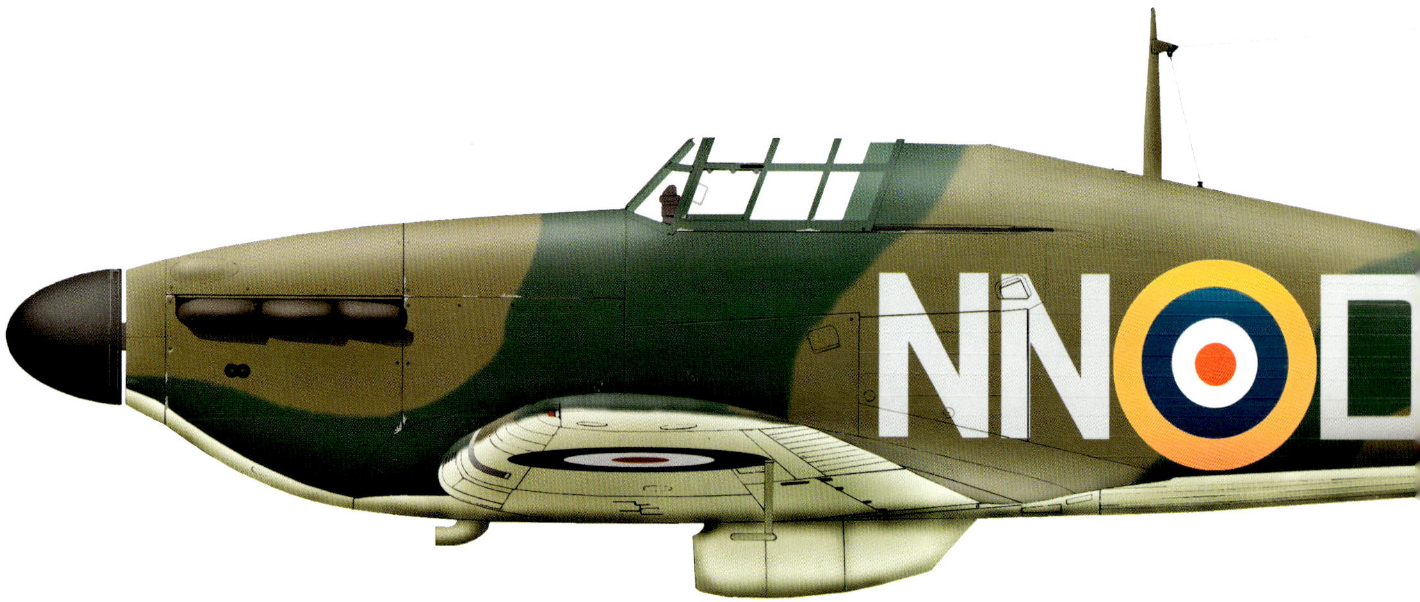

Technical Information Hurricane I:
Length: 9.58 m. Wingspan: 12.20 m. Wing area: 23.97 m2. Gross weight: approx. 3 020 kg. Maximum speed: approx. 510 kph at 5 400 m.2 Rate of climb: 730 m/min. Service ceiling: approx. 10 500 m. Range: approx. 680 km. Power Plant: one liquid-cooled Rolls-Royce Merlin V-12 engine producing 1,030 h.p. Armament: eight .303 inch Browning machine-guns in the wings.

Hawker Hurricane Mk. I, NN-D, of the Czechoslovakian No. 310 Squadron formed at Duxford on 10 July 1940. The Hurricane is generally considered to have been inferior to the Bf 109. It could, however, outturn the Messerschmitt and was able to absorb more battle damage. The aircraft was simple to fly and maintain and provided a good weapons platform. When possible, Hurricanes attacked the German bombers while Spitfires tackled the Bf 109s. Almost two-thirds of Fighter Command squadrons were equipped with the Hurricane in the summer of 1940.

Replica of the Bf 109 E-4 flown by Helmut Wick as *Gruppenkommandeur*. It is one of three replicas made of fiberglass and original parts on display in the Battle of Britain Museum in Folkestone. The museum also has a Hurricane, a Spitfire and a huge collection of recovered artifacts from that period. The museum is housed in an original building of a former RAF airfield. When photographed in 1993, the replica, still without wings, was parked in the corner of a hangar. This unfortunately not particularly authentic piece may by now have found a more worthy place in the expansion of the museum.

The book *Helmut Wick – Das Leben eines Fliegerhelden* was published in two different editions by the *Luftwaffe* magazine *Der Adler*, beginning in 1943. On the right a biography that appeared in 1941.